WE NEED
TO TALK

WE NEED
TO TALK

WE NEED TO TALK

Living With the Afterlife

LYN RAGAN

HourGlass Publishing
ATLANTA, GA

Cover Image: *Ioannis Gousgounis,* Athens, Greece
Book and Cover Design by *Lynn M Oney*
Tradepaper ISBN 978-0-6159808-2-9

HOURGLASS PUBLISHING
2095 Highway 211 NW, Suite 2F-152
Braselton, GA 30517
info@hourglasspublishing.com
www.hourglasspublishing.com

Printed in the United States of America

This book is dedicated to the one I love, Chip Oney.
He made an enormous difference in my life in so
many ways when he was here in the physical
world, as he continues to do so even
today … from the
Other Side.
Thank you, my darling, for sharing your amazing love.

Other Books By Lyn Ragan

WAKE ME UP! A True Story
Love and The Afterlife

BERC'S Inner Voice
(Children's Book)
Author, Lyn Ragan
Illustrator, Alison Meyer

Contents

This is a true story. Some names, places, and other identifying details were changed to protect individual privacy. The timing of events was compressed to facilitate the telling of the story.

No part of this book is intended for educational purposes. This story is about this author's personal experiences. Please keep in mind that no two people experience the same communications—they are as individual as humans are.

Part 1

New Beginning's

When one life ends, another begins…

T he future is an absolute unknown. When staring into the eyes of a complete stranger for the first time, the last thing imagined is unspeakable tragedy.

The moment I gazed into Chip's eyes, an undeniable burst of sparks hit me like a ton of bricks. A warning of sorts. "Stay away!" It was mandatory. If I didn't, a very big change would come and I knew it.

At that time, I thought the strange emotions stirring up were because I was married. As luck would have it though, I found myself headed directly into the line of fire making a beeline straight to a divorce. It wasn't a secret that my twelve year marriage wasn't healthy. Living in separate bedrooms, however, was entirely too easy to get accustomed to.

I was very comfortable and to be honest, I don't like change. It was much easier to stay put and secure than it was to head into something unknown.

As for the new stranger, this man who had eyes that

burned a hole into my ever-sinking heart, I vowed I wasn't ready for a new relationship. It had been fourteen years since I'd been single and I needed to find *me* again. Somehow, I had lost myself so badly into what someone else wanted me to be, that I had forgotten my own likes and dislikes. Whatever was to happen down the road was certainly going to happen, I instinctively knew that, but I also knew I had to put my foot down too… no darn relationship.

Well, that all lasted a whopping three months or so after my separation. Chip—with his beautiful, sparkling, ocean blue eyes—was no stranger to going after someone he took a liking to. He was a persistent little pest.

I did hold true to the one thing I knew I had to accomplish though: no serious relationship. During the first year of our courtship, time had a way of standing in between us for a day or two after we went out. It was easy to stay on course. I don't know why we did that—let time stand in the way—it wasn't something either of us asked for or even planned, it just happened. But that space of time allowed me to think of other things. To be blunt, it allowed me to keep my feelings in check and not fall *in love* with him.

But, oh my gosh, did I ever enjoy the heck out of Chip's company. Only a couple of weeks into our friendship and I swore I had known him my entire life. We quickly became best friends and literally could talk about anything. Well, anything other than a couple of rules he put in place from the get go.

One, we weren't allowed to discuss religion. And two, no politics. He said by us discussing these two topics, our relationship might fall into fleeting waters and he didn't want that to happen. It didn't really bother me. I wasn't a religious person, but I did believe in a higher power. At a very young age, I knew that someone lied about Mary Magdalene being a prostitute... and I believed in Jesus, too. But religious in the sense that I attended church? No, I knew I could talk to God all on my own.

As for politics, I was never up-to-date on that subject. I didn't watch much television, what with finding the new me and all, because I didn't have the time. What we did discuss was everything else from the sun to the moon and back.

Chip was a strong talker. By learning what triggered him... why... it became quite pleasurable to ask him a question and then sit back for a while and listen to his voice, to his non-fancy vocabulary, and hear the pure excitement that came from the deepest innerness of his mind, his passionate self. I thoroughly enjoyed him and everything that came with him.

The telephone became our means to communicate. We practically lived on it. I suppose having the jobs we had allowed us the freedom to carry on the way we did. The last two years it was nothing to see our minutes go over 14,000 each month. That was an insane amount of time on the phone, but it became our norm. If we went below 9,000, he accused me of not loving him anymore.

Before I knew it, years had passed. Nothing had progressed in our relationship in regards to making a forever life commitment, and I was quite happy with the way we were. No strings, no ties, no fears, no nothing really where the heart was concerned. Yet, I would've done anything in the world for him. I had no friend like the one I had in Chip.

He was an amazing man.

He was a riot to be around, a romantic at heart, a lover of life, had a personality to die for; he was perfect in every way. But, he let so much time go by without pressing or pushing me forward, I became too complacent in how we were... care free.

And then, one afternoon, I found myself talking to him on

the phone, waiting for my lunch to get ready. We were carrying on and laughing, when out of the blue he questioned me about something that shook me wide awake.

He asked, "Are you in love with me, Lynnie?"

I had no idea how to answer his question. He had placed me in a quandary and hurting his feelings was the last thing I wanted to do. Yet, I knew I had to tell him the truth... no, I wasn't *in* love with him. I gathered up some courage and *prayed* I didn't crush him.

"I do love you, Chip. But I don't think I'm *in* love with you," I delivered, as delicately as I could.

"You're not in love with me?" His disappointment broke my heart.

"Sweetie, I do love you," I told him. "You are my very best friend. I think because we spend so much time on the phone and not in person, we haven't given ourselves the opportunity to grow together, at least not emotionally."

And then there it was. That God-awful sound of silence. He didn't say a single, solitary word for what felt like a lifetime. So I decided to ask *him* the same question. "Are you in love with me, Chip?"

Again, there was nothing but the stillness of the moment and my heart sank to my feet. This wonderful man spoke louder through his silence than with any words he could have possibly said. I had done it again. I hurt his feelings. Since I often had a knack for saying the wrong things and always at the right time, I raced to a quick response.

"Chip, let me try to explain how Lyn operates. Maybe then you'll understand where I come from. In order for me to give you my heart in love, not the friendly or brotherly kind, you have to spend time with me... in person. You have to grab my attention, you have to caress my heart, you have to look me in the eyes when you talk to me, and you have to hold my hand when I need you. Chip, we haven't spent a lot of time together doing something other than... well, you know."

"I know, darlin," he whispered softly. They were his first words in what seemed like hours, and I suddenly felt a significant pull to reassure him.

"Can I see myself *falling* in love with you, Chip? Yes, I can," I told him. "I've kept myself from doing that because I thought this was what you wanted, too. This weird but fantastic arrangement between us."

"You *can* see yourself falling in love with me?" he asked, with the cutest tone.

"Yes, of course. But it won't happen overnight."

I worried about putting ideas in his head.

Like so many of our conversations past, he changed the subject entirely. This one though, weighed heavy on my mind. I had no idea what he was looking for. Or if in fact he was *in love* with me, or if love was a road he truly wanted to travel. I knew I could talk to him about it if I wanted to, but I refused to bring the subject up...refused with **big and bold** capital letters. In some way, I wished for it to all quietly go away.

I loved our relationship with a passion. I loved who we were together and I absolutely loved, not having to worry if I was going to have another failed relationship. Two marriages down and I seriously didn't want another. What Chip and I shared was safe and so much fun.

Why in the world would he want to go and change that?

But that's exactly what he did. He changed *us*. It didn't take long for him to alter who we were together. In barely weeks, everything we had built together changed and all of a sudden, we were joined at the hip. Remarkably, it felt extremely normal and surprisingly wonderful.

I started thinking about him more than I ever had. I missed the heck out of him when we weren't together. I looked forward to his calls and to seeing him pull up in my driveway. I daydreamed of our future together. Everything was changing and it was all happening so *scary* fast.

Before I knew it, I was head over heels in love with Chip and terrified to admit it. Oftentimes, I stared into his eyes and wondered if he had an ulterior motive, or questioned if he was playing a game with my emotions. I debated if he was real and then pinched myself to make sure that *I* was. He was too perfect and to be honest, a part of me didn't feel like I deserved someone so special.

Because of that, every few months it seemed, I made stuff up (lies) inside my head and forced myself to believe them. Breaking up became a priority. Something within told me our relationship was bad for me, yet everything about us felt amazingly perfect. I couldn't figure out what it was that really bugged me, or scared me, so badly when I looked at him. Every time I attempted to end our relationship though, I backed out or he did something silly to change my mind.

The last of those episodes was shortly after Scooby, our Lab puppy, came into our lives. Sitting on the coffee table, I was trying to convince Chip that we couldn't be together. He was standing in front of me cradling Scooby in his arms, rocking him back and forth like a little baby. His eyes lifted to meet mine and more serious than ever, he said, "If we get a divorce, our son will be ruined for life." I couldn't do anything but laugh because that was just the dumbest thing I'd ever heard him say.

In that instant, I knew I didn't want to go through with kicking him out of my life. I started grilling what it was I was trying to do and when I examined the past, it was obvious:

every few months something took over me and a huge feeling of worry crept in. It would scream at me loudly, "You have to protect yourself! He's going to hurt you!"

Yet, I knew he'd never hurt a fly.

How could I break up with Chip when I had no *real* reason to do so? How might I end our relationship when I loved him dearly? It was a strong force telling me to get out before it was too late, but I always argued back, "Too late for what?"

The urgency to stop loving him drove me crazy.

January 2008 brought with it new promises. Another year had come full circle and there we were, stronger in our love than ever. I did a lot of work on *me* and had finally stopped worrying. I quit trying to figure out what was wrong; which for someone like me, that was huge. I wanted to be grateful for what I had and thankful for receiving such a miraculous kind of love. I was *mesmerized* by this man.

When he picked up my hand and touched it with his lips, his tender kiss sent shivers through my body. When he lifted my head to gaze into his eyes and then slowly and gently kissed my lips, my whole body melted. When he soared into bed like Superman and then softly pressed himself against me, I fell deeper in love with him. He had me... hook, line, and sinker.

A couple of weeks into January, I had an amazing epiphany. Sitting under the bright sun one afternoon, a strong *knowing* came over me. "This love will last forever."

I heard it so clearly. It was one of those warm sensation feelings that carried with it an instant understanding. *Chip would be in my life until the day I died.* I was now convinced we'd be together always.

Even more amazing than that perception, was an immediate release of the strange urgency to break up with him.

Instead, I could see our future clearly. We were going to be great together. And because I believed it so emphatically, I did a complete one hundred and eighty degree turn.

Letting go of so much fear was invigorating. To be able to receive love, and allow him to love me the way he wanted was astounding, and freeing, all at the same time. My entire perspective of *us* had changed.

Finally, after years of struggle and harmful relationships, we were coming together quite nicely. For the first time in my life, I felt peace, at home in my skin, and loved. I was truly surprised to experience what it felt like to *feel* love. And more importantly, to *be* loved. Life couldn't be any better. I was more than blessed, I was in *heaven*.

But then … something horrible happened …

Part 2

The Ending

Dying is slow and very painful...

JANUARY 23, 2008

I would have never thought it. Not in a million years. To wake up to the sound of love, only to experience unspeakable tragedy minutes later... it was clearly a day that would change our lives forever.

At 4:33 a.m. my phone rang. Startled, I shot out of bed. I was always up by four o'clock, but today, I was late. The phone was sitting on a table across the room. I ran over to pick it up and then answered, sweetly.

"Good morning, my sweetie pie."

"Good morning, baby doll," my lover said, enthusiastically.

I adored our early morning calls; my daily dose of love.

While I pretended to be up a few minutes prior to him calling, I moved through the house to let the fur-kids out to potty. I walked outside, watched our dogs do their duties, and while my sweetheart talked about the night before, I marched back inside.

Chip was sharing how bad he felt. Because of his irritating cough, he said he wasn't able to get much sleep. Meanwhile, I brought down one of our new cups he insisted we buy for Christmas. I placed it on the counter next to the coffee pot, turned on the machine, and waited for the brewing to end.

We were both fighting a terrible cold. Chip had an early day at work planned. Yesterday, we decided to take some time off to play. I would leave work at noon, meet him at home, we'd hop in the new car we bought last week, and go for a ride.

"That'll make us feel better," he said. But today, he doesn't sound so good. In fact, he sounded horrible.

"You're probably not going to feel like going later, are you?" I asked him. I thought he might say no, so I was surprised when he replied, "Let's wait to see how I feel when that time gets here, okay?"

As we talked on his way to work, I pictured him perfectly sitting in the driver's seat of his big red Dually Dodge. I knew he was holding his maroon Starbucks coffee mug in his right hand, while resting his arm on the middle console. His left hand was hanging over the top of the steering wheel while he talked through the Bluetooth connected to his left ear.

I didn't hear him stop to unlock the gate. Nor did I hear him take the cooler from his pickup and put it into his semi. What I did hear—was him starting the big truck. I heard the sound of the engine turn over and I knew with certainty I said, "I heard you start her up, sweetie."

"Yep, we started her up," I know he replied.

I then pictured him hopping down out of the semi needing to start his pre-trip inspection. He never skipped that part of his routine. But on this one morning, he only took one or two steps forward before our lives changed forever.

At this moment in time, I knew nothing.

Once I heard the truck start, I imagined him still sitting inside realizing something went wrong. The reason I assumed this was that only seconds later, at approximately 4:45 a.m., his voice growled out two big words.

"Oh shit!"

I instantly thought something wasn't quite right with the truck and I asked, "What's wrong, sweetie?"

But he didn't reply.

I then pictured him getting out of the truck to check the engine. I knew that was the first place he'd go. He'd have to release the latches on each side of the hood in order to lift it.

But how did he do that so fast?

What I heard next was a horrific, loud sound blasting through the phone. So much so that I had to take it away from my ear. I couldn't hear anything but a horrible noise that sounded like a lawnmower engine. It was deafening. It was difficult to fathom anything under the hood being that loud, but again, I still didn't know anything.

I asked once again, "Sweetie, what's wrong with the truck?"

How can he hear me if I can't hear him?

Through the loud noise though, I continued to ask, shouting now. "Chip, can you hear me?"

Something felt so wrong. As I paced back and forth in my living room, I decided he needed my help. I ran into the kitchen and grabbed my keys off the counter. At that exact moment, the sound of the lawnmower engine slowly tempered off.

"Sweetie, is everything all right? Are you okay?"

But I got nothing back.

Suddenly, I heard what I thought was Chip sniffling. I knew then he was still on the phone.

Why isn't he talking to me? Is he playing a bad game?

I asked yet again, "Sweetie pie, are you all right?"

No words came through my ear.

I charged out the front door, leaving the dogs in the house, and raced to my car. I listened intently for anything he might say. At the same time I reassured him I was on my way to help him. I lived less than two miles from where he parked; it wouldn't take me long to get there.

"I'm on my way, sweetie. I don't know what's wrong, but I'm coming to help, okay? You're not talking to me darlin', and you're starting to scare me."

I could hear him breathing, but he never said a word.

"Are you okay, sweetie?"

I flew down Normandy Boulevard hitting seventy-five and eighty miles per hour in a thirty mile per hour zone. It never dawned on me to slow down.

"You need to say something, darlin'. Why aren't you talking to me, Chip?" My heart was racing now and my legs were shaking uncontrollably. Fear had creeped in.

There was a lot of traffic out to be so early in the morning. At one point, I got stuck at a red light where I sat behind a white work truck listening to Chip's breathing in my ear. My mind was racing wild fast.

"Sweetie, do I need to hang up and call 911? Can you talk to me? You're scaring me, Chip. I don't know what's wrong. Please say something to me. Please, Chip, say anything."

Still, no words echoed through my ear.

"As soon as I get around this truck I'm there, sweetie."

I sped through the last light before arriving at the lot.

"I'm right here, darlin'. I'm turning into the driveway right now, coming to you. I am right here!"

I saw the lights shining across the lot from his truck. The driveway was bumpy as I passed the office buildings on the main road. It was so damn *dark* out.

"I'm here, sweetie. Where are you?"

And then, my eyes found him. I could see him off in the distance lying on the ground next to his truck.

"Oh my God, oh my God!" I yelled.

I heard those words flying all around my head in the thick air, over and over again. They had nowhere to escape.

My foot stomped the gas pedal as I rushed to his side.

I stopped not directly in front of him, but more off to the right. When I slammed the car into park and sought for him to move, I noticed streaks of blood running across his forehead. I knew I had to get help fast. I jumped out and ran toward the road. But then I thought, *is he still alive?*

I turned around and ran back. I searched to see if his chest was moving up and down.

Oh, thank God, he's alive!

Disturbingly though, I saw a large hole in the back of his head. I rapidly concluded that he must have fallen off of the truck somehow and hurt himself. There was so much blood.

I knew I had to calm myself down and shut off my thoughts. It was imperative I help him. Getting off the phone was the first step.

"I have to hang up now, sweetie, so I can call 911. I'll be right back. Okay? I promise!"

I hit the end button and disconnected us. I saw the blue light blink twice by his head, glowing brightly through the darkness. He could no longer hear my voice and that worried me.

I turned and ran as fast as I could. It was vital I had the physical address to get help, fast. At the same time I dialed.

4:53 a.m. — I pressed 911, but it didn't go through. I tried again, but got nothing. I called "0," and again, I got no tone whatsoever.

13

4:54 a.m. — I dialed 411. I gave city and state information. An operator answered. I told her I needed 911, but now she was gone, too. It felt like a lifetime before a voice answered I was unable to register.

I had long reached the road and was waiting in front of the mailbox, staring directly at the property numbers.

I shouted, "Is this 911?"

She responded, "Yes."

Instantly, I yelled it out.

"I need an ambulance at 9501 Normandy Boulevard."

I repeated it two more times with complete verbal accuracy and no southern drawl. I insisted on having no mental errors. There could be no mistakes.

I remember the 911 operator asking me questions about my relationship with Chip and after I answered, I made sure to tell her about the large hole in the back of his head.

In my fogginess, all I could think about was how we needed help immediately. I don't think I said it out loud, though. And then, out of nowhere, she put a man on the phone.

He asked if Chip was still breathing.

"I don't know," I told him. "I came out here to the road to get the address. I'm going back right now."

I ran to Chip as quickly as I could. While I was running, I glanced at his truck. The hood wasn't raised. It was intact as though nothing had been touched.

Why didn't I see that before?

I hurriedly tried to piece it all together.

So he didn't go under the hood? What was that noise then? How'd he get hurt? He must've fallen off the truck and hit something. *That's it, he fell.*

Once I was beside him, I repeated it again to the 911 operator. "He has a large hole in the back of his head."

His head was resting in a mud puddle combined with a large amount of his blood. I couldn't tell if it was brain matter or if it was bone lying right underneath his head. I walked around him and squatted on the left side of his body. I stared at his face noting how calm he appeared and then I watched him breathe.

His chest moved up and then slowly down. He appeared to be asleep, yet snoring loudly. I'd watched him sleep many times before—it was exactly how he looked now.

There were streaks of blood that made crisscross marks across the top of his head.

How did you get these blood marks, Chip? They're odd. And I don't see anything else on your face.

I'd mentioned Chip's snoring to the man on the phone. He told me he was gasping for air.

And then he said, "I'm going to tell you what you need to do to help him breathe easier until help arrives. I will instruct you step-by-step."

First, he said I'd have to lift Chip's head back by placing my hand under his neck. I did. I buried my hand in the mud and pushed as far as I could under his neck, and then I tried to lift him.

He didn't move. I couldn't budge him. He was so heavy. The man told me again I needed to lift his head back to open his airways, so I kept trying.

I placed my phone on top of his stomach and I positioned myself above him with my hands under his neck. With both hands now locked, I lifted with all my might.

I still couldn't move him. His head seemed to be stuck in the mud.

I picked up the phone and asked the stranger a question.

"Are you sure you want me to do this when the hole on the back of his head is so big?" I was terrified I'd make it worse for Chip and cause him to lose blood faster.

I don't think the man replied to my question, or either I don't remember what he said. The next thing I heard was him telling me I needed to clean out Chip's mouth so he wouldn't choke on anything.

By this time, my hands were downright muddy. The only thing I could think of was putting all that mud inside of his mouth. I wiped my hands on my clothes and tried to clean them as much as possible.

I leaned forward, closer to his face, and right when I was about to open his mouth, he took a breath. He scared me and I leaped back.

God, I can't put my filthy fingers in his mouth. I can't make this worse for him than everything already is.

I knew he was breathing because I was sitting there watching him. But I felt totally helpless. I couldn't lift him; he weighed two hundred and twenty-five pounds and was almost double my size. I couldn't budge him, his head wouldn't move.

I was so scared—for him.

"When are they going to be here?" I hollered at the phone.

"They're on the way," the man shouted back.

And then it hit me.

They won't see us! Not back here in this darkness.

I jumped up and ran back to the road.

(If you can picture the size of a football field, imagine me located at the one yard line standing on Normandy while Chip is located at the fifty.)

Everything felt like it was taking forever.

I paced back and forth on the dark road, looking for lights to appear. There were none. It wasn't long before I heard that stranger's voice again. He asked if Chip was still breathing. I had to confess I'd returned to the road to wait for the ambulance.

"You need to help Chip; you need to go back to him," he told me firmly.

I turned and ran. Never questioning if he was right or wrong. *I know they won't see us. It's too dark out.*

But I ran anyway. Chip needed me with him.

I squatted down in the identical spot where I was before.

I laid my hand on top of his tummy; I needed to be touching him. While we waited, this time I looked around. I glanced to the right and peered behind me at the truck.

I saw no blood anywhere on the back of it and I couldn't see where he would have fallen either. There was no disturbance on the ground below or around the immediate area of his truck. I then studied Chip from head to toe, observing him stretched out in front of me.

He was wearing his Gator Football blue and orange sweat shirt with his khaki-colored shorts. I saw his white ankle socks and his dark brown leather work shoes, too. He was lying flat on his back with his legs slightly parted and his arms were out to his side. His coffee mug had fallen out of his hand and it was resting right beside him in the wet grass.

I didn't see anything out of the ordinary. The only lights upon us were the ones from my car headlights and they were sitting at an angle. The moon was bright above us, but it wasn't illuminating enough to see anything clearly.

I watched him sleep. There was nothing else I could do but sit with him in the darkness… and wait. I leaned over and kissed his cheek, his eyes, his head, and I told him I loved him.

I rubbed his cheek with my hand and I begged him, "Just hang on, sweetie, they're on their way. They'll be here soon. Just hang on."

But inside I was screaming it at the top of my lungs, *please*

17

hang on, my love! Please don't leave me!

Lights were beaming through the trees. Finally. They were here. I hollered into the phone. "Tell them to turn now! Make a right-hand turn now or they'll miss our road."

I sat there and watched them drive past us. Another rescue unit went by, and then another. My voice cracked in its determination to control the situation.

"Tell them to make a U-turn and then make another one to come right back here," I screamed.

I could hear him talking, but not to me. I waited for them to return, but they didn't. Too much time had gone by. I realized it then, they didn't make that second U-turn.

"Where are they? They didn't come back," I yelled.

I knew time was critical. I was beyond terrified. This was all taking so long. I knew we were teetering on the edge of saving Chip's life.

I jumped up and ran as fast as I could. It had rained all night long, so I hit every puddle on the dirt road leading back to Normandy. My pajama pants were soaked with mud.

When I reached the highway, I couldn't see a rescue unit anywhere. They were gone. They vanished. The road was pitch-black. It was as though I had closed my eyes and become blind.

I screamed into the phone, "Where are they? Where did they go?"

The stranger's voice wasn't as calm as it was earlier. He convincingly responded, "They're trying to find you!"

"Oh, wait," I shouted. "I can see them."

I saw the lights appearing from a good distance down the road. Before I knew which way they would turn though, I fell.

My knees hit the pavement, hard; they gave out. I found myself praying, begging—desperately pleading—out loud.

"Please tell them to come back this way. Tell them to please, please, please... come back this way."

I could feel the pounding of my heart inside my head now. It was taking everything I had to stay focused.

I watched as the lights slowly crossed the median. *Yes!* They were heading toward us. I counted to three as they all turned in our direction. As calmly as I could, I waited for their arrival.

Right before they reached me though, a police car appeared out of nowhere. It was in the left-hand lane next to the rescue unit leading the way. The flashing neon blue of its lights were reflecting all over the dark. I sensed the speed it was traveling, fast. And when a bright light shined upon me, I couldn't help but wave frantically.

I imagined what they saw: a woman on the side of the road in the middle of nowhere. She had wild hair and mud-covered pajamas, jumping up and down, waving her arms madly.

"This way, this way!" I screamed.

I knew they couldn't hear my pleas for them to hurry. They were still too far away, but I hollered it out anyway.

The first rescue pulled into the driveway. I told them to go straight back to the right side of the lot, and Chip would be on the other side of my car.

"You will see him," I yelled.

I stood stock-still as they one-by-one drove by. I waited until the police car passed, too. I'd forgotten all about the man on the phone when I pulled my cell back to my ear to see if he was still there.

"Hello?"

"Are they there?" the stranger asked, "I want to make sure they're there before we hang up."

I confirmed.

I ran, fast. Back to Chip. It was now 5:10 a.m. There were

three rescue units and one police car by his side. My heart was racing so fast from fear, from running; it felt as though it was going to explode out of my chest. I couldn't control my breathing.

But I kept observing. I watched them all around Chip. The police officer walked over and asked me questions about him like his name, phone number, address, etc., for the next few minutes.

I then tried getting closer to see what they were doing, but the officer told me I needed to step back. He then told me they were going to airlift Chip to Shands Hospital.

A few minutes later, I realized I needed to call his mom. At 5:19 a.m. I dialed Chip's house, but his mother didn't answer. At that exact moment, the police officer walked back over.

"How's he doing?" I asked him. "How'd he get hurt?"

He told me Chip was unconscious. But as soon as I understood what he said, I heard him say something else.

"He's been shot."

My knees went weak again and I fell straight to the ground, shrieking out loud. "Shot? How in the hell did he get shot?"

I didn't really expect an explanation from the officer. I was in total disbelief. It didn't feel real.

I had already pressed the button to re-dial and this time Chip's mom answered. Her sleepy voice danced across my ear.

"Char, this is Lyn. Are you awake enough for me to talk to you?"

"Yeah, sweetie. What's wrong?"

I proceeded to tell her the police informed me her son had been shot and she needed to get to the hospital. I stayed on the phone with her until she got dressed.

And then, I moved closer to Chip. Again, the cop told me I needed to step over to my car. So I did.

I watched as they cut his Gator shirt from his chest. He was bare-chested, but thankfully I could see it moving up and down with his breathing. One of the EMTs brought over a stretcher and this was when I noticed their dilemma. They had to figure out a way to move him.

Three men grabbed his feet and yanked him from the puddle of blood he was in—they tugged and jerked his body so hard, his head bounced high into the air and then hit the ground with a hard thump. My hands immediately clutched the sides of my face when I screamed in silence, "Oh my God, how can they do that? They're hurting him!"

I later learned he was literally stuck in the mud. The first gunshot into his nose sent him sailing straight back. His head sank into the mud bonding him like a suction cup. Brute strength was the only way to pull him out.

I still felt safe in the thought that they were going to take care of him. Silently, I tried to convince myself, "He's in good hands now. They can save him. They will save him!"

The officer took me to his car and told me I needed to sit inside until everything was taken care of. I did as he said. I knew he was tired of telling me to get back. I couldn't blame him. I had no more strength left in me anyway. I was mentally and emotionally spent.

From where I sat inside the police car, I could see Chip perfectly. As they were about to lift him into the rescue, I watched his bare chest continue to move up and down. I could see they had placed an air mask over his face and had put his neck in a brace, too.

The officer told me airlifting Chip to the hospital was a good sign. They have hope they'll be able to save him.

Stay alive, sweetie, I prayed. We'll conquer anything and everything. You just need to stay alive, my darling.

It felt like hours had passed. He needed to get to the hospital and I couldn't figure out why they hadn't left yet. I watched everyone like a hawk.

My mind was racing fast. I had literally hundreds of thoughts flashing all at the same time. I couldn't help it. I was locating answers for Chip. I knew he wasn't going to like having scars.

"It doesn't matter what it looks like, we will make sure we fix it so you don't think it'll be ugly," I talked to him inside my head. "There's no worry there, my love."

I assumed he was going to have bad headaches, too. Hell, he had a hole in the back of his head the size of a silver dollar. But I found an answer for that as well. I imagined myself whispering it into his ear.

"Modern medicine will take care of this also, my love. We will make it through whatever we have to. Keep fighting. I'll be right there by your side the entire way. As soon as they let me out of here, I'm on my way. I promise."

I pressed my hands on the car window and smashed my face against the glass. My eyes attacked the stretcher under his head—it was covered, completely, in red.

He was still losing a lot of blood.

Yet, I still sat there hoping against all hope he'd be okay. He would survive. I knew Chip. He was the perfect portrait of a real fighter.

They lifted him up and pushed him inside the rescue. The doors slammed shut and my heart sank. I watched as they backed up and drove away. I could hear the helicopter off in the distance too. I knew exactly when they flew by. Chip loved helicopters. I couldn't imagine that being his last ride in one. We had so much to look forward to. We had so much more to accomplish in our lives together.

Silence.

That was all that surrounded me now. Two police officers and I sat in this God-forsaken pitch black lot in complete, deep and gloomy silence.

I was confined to the back seat of a police car. I had never felt so alone in all of my life. I was petrified for Chip. I couldn't even think of him not surviving.

"Why are they keeping me here? Why won't they let me go to my fiancé? What about the dogs, are they okay?"

"What about work? What will I say? I didn't lock the front door. What if someone breaks in the house and hurts the dogs? I need to go home. I need to get out of here; I need to be with Chip."

My mind was all over the place.

"God, I pray he's okay. How am I going to find out? I hope Char took her phone with her. Should I call his dad and tell him what happened this morning? No. Char will take care of that. I need to get out of this car. Why are they keeping me here?"

My thoughts continued to ramble in my head.

"Oh hell, they think I did this, don't they? But how can they possibly think I'd have anything to do with shooting him? This man is my entire existence."

"What will I do without him if he dies?"

I prayed out loud, "Oh God, please don't let him die. Please take care of Chip, God. Please don't let this be his time. I beg of you, please don't take Chip from me…please!"

There was no concept of time. I knew I needed to get away soon, though. I wanted Chip to know I was trying to get there as fast as I could. He needed me. I should've been allowed to go with him.

Does he know I'm not there?

Seeing all that blood he lost and watching him breath, I

couldn't visualize anything else. And my thoughts, they were on a fast track to nowhere.

"He's been shot. Someone shot Chip. It doesn't make sense. None of this makes sense. It can't be real."

"Someone shot Chip!"

I shook my head hard, trying to figure everything out.

"But I'm here, sitting in this cop car where I shouldn't be. I know this can't be happening. It can't possibly be real. There should be a way to start this day all over."

"Maybe I'm still sleeping and all of this is a bad dream."

I figured Chip's mom would be at the hospital now, so I dialed her cell. All of this had to be a bad dream, a horrible nightmare. It couldn't be real, because the next thing I heard was unimaginable.

"Lyn, no, Chip passed away a few minutes ago. He's gone."

On this damp, dark, dreary, ugly Wednesday morning, our lives changed forever.

The love of my life, Christopher J. Oney, died.

My sweet, sweet Chip … was murdered.

Part 3

Grief vs. Belief

To survive takes a leap of faith…

I couldn't for the life of me wrap my head around Chip's murder. I couldn't believe for a second that he was dead. And to think I'd never talk to him again was inconceivable.

I had never felt so lost in all my life. I had never known such overwhelming guilt, horrendous sadness, such painful heartbreak, and horrid pain as I did after his death. The first few months were the worst, deadly bad, but the subsequent months and the ensuing years were painful too… it was just the magnitude of that pain was downgraded by a degree or two.

Somehow, Chip came back to life. As soon as he transformed into his spirit-self, he went directly to work. And as strange as that sounds, that's truly what he did.

Chip saved my life for the second time and he did it from that place we call *the other side*.

I knew I was going to face death someday, but I never, ever, imagined facing it this way. To be honest, I never had a reason to think about death or the afterlife for that matter. With the exception of my brother, Billy, all of my family was still living. Billy's funeral was the only one I had ever attended, in the late 80s, and back then, the afterlife was a dot in the spectrum of what life had in store for me.

When I heard those horrible words screech through my ear, *No Lyn, he's gone...* my breath was literally stolen. My heart was ripped from my chest as I watched it being propelled into the wind vanishing into infinite dust. Everything inside of me disappeared, with Chip. I became a walking, lifeless, inanimate body with no spirit inside.

My sadness was as big as the sky and I prayed every day to die. I knew I'd never take my own life, but I earnestly begged for Chip to take me. When he didn't retrieve me, I then turned to God and begged – day after day after day.

I had no physical strength or emotional energy to accomplish anything. I was so devastated and utterly *dead* inside; all I could do was cry. The only thing I longed for and desperately needed, was to be wherever Chip was.

But Chip would have none of that.

He decided that I needed to become one of those people who experience vivid dreams; also known as a *night traveler* or a *dream walker*. At first, I had no idea my dreams would later be defined as Afterlife Visitations, Dream-Visits, or ADC's *(After Death Communication)*. Yet, I quickly understood that either, one, I was going insane; or two, something extraordinary was happening.

He visited me non-stop for months and documenting what happened became a full-time job. Little did I know that with his death, my life would become an endless hesitation of confusing and unreal events amid nightly visits while I slept.

For much of the first two years, I became completely

unaware of what reality I lived in—awake within a dream or living my normal everyday life. This other world was so real that my human existence became less important than my sleeping life.

The enormous amount of comfort I felt from seeing him, from hearing his voice, or from feeling his arms hold me and hug me, it all delivered a sense of peace within that words can't begin to describe. It was incredible. Chip was showing me that he was as alive as you and I sitting here today.

There were lots of other things, too, like bumps in the night or knocking on my walls; always three it seemed. There were items moved from one place to another, like my keys taken from inside my car and moved to the kitchen counter. Or finding a seed in the bathroom sink, or locating an object in the middle of the floor, or witnessing a white bead dropped into my closed hand, or seeing butterflies at the most opportune moments. The biggest connection we had though—and still have—is music.

Somehow, Chip manipulated my thoughts and inserted a lyric or two—I could hear the artist singing the song—and as quickly as it danced across my mind, I acknowledged it. I then dashed to the internet to locate the song and always found a very special message of love. Soon, I began calling them my *messages of love from the Afterlife*. Or I said I'd been *kissed again from the other side*.

I understand now that it was a magical beginning. It was a hard-to-believe and very sad start filled to the brim with grief, no doubt about that, but it was also an amazing experience loaded with mystery and intrigue.

Since Chip's death, my view on physical reality and all that it meant to me changed. I knew I could never go back to the person I was before, and gradually, *faith* started to play an enormous role. The most important lesson in my journey of surviving Chip's murder was learning the meaning of that one word, *faith*.

This word grew to be a very powerful source in my life and quickly became my link to the other side. For me, it became more about trusting a new belief system that was much larger than me—Chip was really alive.

From that magnificent place on the other side, he shared something wonderful; *we don't die*. Great comfort was found in the *knowing* that life is eternal and a higher power truly exists in which all living things are connected.

We're all capable of being contacted by our deceased loved ones. It doesn't take a special gift to sense their presence or to receive a significant message. It only takes a *leap of faith* to trust *them* and to be open to their many gifts.

It really did help in my grief journey to learn that Chip was always present. As time continued to pass without his physical body, his continued love imprinted its mark inside my heart. To learn that he was aware of everything helped ease my agony and also soothed my desperate need to know if he was happy in his new world.

The most bounteous gift I think I ever received was the moment I finally understood his commitment—I would never be alone again, ever.

Sadly, I never gave any consideration to anyone's feelings after Chip was snatched away so quickly. I was devoured with sadness and I couldn't bear the thought of living without him. On that dark, wet, and dreary morning, I had died too. It was nothing to stare up into the sky, tears streaming down my face, and scream, "Please take me from this evil and dark world."

As much as I begged for that grief-stricken release but experiencing no change in my existence, the heavy rains that poured from my eyes eventually became the fire that drove me. This soon turned into *belief*. While I continued to sob, sometimes uncontrollably, I also understood that something remarkable was happening... the immortality of the soul was being revealed.

When we release these heavy bodies—we survive death.

Even though I couldn't see Chip's spirit-form or hear his physical voice, I still felt him *near*. No matter how painful his death was, in time I learned that everything happens for a reason. As much as I hate admitting that a lesson was learned from our tragic experience, I wouldn't be here today if it hadn't of taken place.

Learning to live without him, physically speaking, is one the hardest things I've ever done. In time, I learned that some lessons in life are invaluable. Even in death, something is always there for the teaching. Chip's death is probably more valuable to me than all of our treasured moments in life.

I also found an answer to that mysterious tug months before he died, the one urging me to end our relationship. Everything finally clicked and made sense... instinctively I knew Chip was going to hurt me. Never would I have thought it though, not in a million years, that he'd hurt me through his murder, my heart vehemently crushed forever. But much later, it made all the sense in the world. My higher-self was preparing me for the inevitable.

Unfortunately we can't change *death*. It's a natural process to life. For those of us who are left behind, the passing of a dear loved one is a life-altering event. My start in experiencing a loss took a toll on me, I won't deny that. But with a tremendous amount of help and love from the Afterlife, I was able to awaken to a new existence.

Dream-visits were a huge part of Chip's communications

the first years. This was where he showed me an abundance of love, as well as his acceptance to where he was. More importantly, he showed me how life continues on once we move past the physical death.

As you read this book, the sequence of events may become a bit confusing as to whether I was truly experiencing the activities in my *real* life, or acting normally within a dream sequence. Welcome to my world.

Chapter Two

Ghost

*Dreams are more real than the
perception of being human.*

My body jerked, my arms flew out, and my knees buckled.
*I had lost control of everything. The impact riddled me
with expansive turmoil.*

*My balance was missing as I stumbled back a few steps.
My breathing skipped a beat as I gasped hard for a breath of
air. My hands slammed hard into my chest pressing firmly
against my heart. Every thought had vanished while I rocked
with sudden confusion.*

"What the hell was that?" I screamed out.

*It happened so quickly. So fast that I never got the chance
to see who it was, or what it was, that flew inside of me with
such a force. All I knew, it was still inside of me.*

*My heart was beating a million miles a minute and my feet
were super-glued to the floor. I was scared to death. I could
feel it, I could feel my body frozen in place.*

*My eyes could move though, so I darted them from left to
right, right to left, trying like crazy to find help. I didn't want to
panic, I really didn't, but I was on the verge of snapping.*

I was too scared to move, yet I could feel my body

trembling and shaking hard. "Am I freezing?" I asked myself. "No, I'm not cold," I found myself answering. "It has to be this something else causing me to shake so badly."

"Should I scream for help? I wonder if Chip will hear me. Will he be able to help me?"

I stood stiffly still, quietly waiting. The seconds felt like hours. Nothing was happening and nothing was changing.

"Oh dear God, what if I'm not okay?! What have I done?" I questioned. "And why is this happening?"

"Only minutes ago I was sitting with Chip," I tried hard to remember. "Wasn't I?"

I allowed myself to travel back to those earlier moments when I lifted my head, little by little, shaking off the apparent grogginess. The vision in front of me was a little hazy, but I swore I was looking at a bald spot on top of a man's head. As I stared at it for the longest time, it finally sunk in. Indeed, I was gazing at strands of blond hair, glistening with little beads of sparkling sweat.

My arms embraced the naked head, knowing exactly who it belonged to. Automatically and very slowly, my hands caressed the silky, baby fine hair. And then, I pulled him closer to my chest while I wrapped my arms around his neck, holding him tightly in place.

I had decided to take a look around and turned my head to the right. An amazingly bright green couch was sitting there. Its color was like an exquisite emerald stone, strikingly beautiful. The texture looked as silky as a bed of velvety smooth flowers. And then I whispered something about three people being able to sit there quite nicely.

Out of the corner of my eye, I saw the edge of my leg. When I started to focus on it, my thoughts hit me like a bolt of lightning. "Holy cow, I'm sitting in the middle of this green couch. *Where the hell am I?"*

Instantaneously, the darkness of the room grabbed my attention. It was difficult to see anything, but far off to the right I could make out a centuries old mantle. The red bricks that made up the fireplace were aged, faded, and worn out from extensive use. Even the mortar had all but disappeared, yet it was still being used because a pile of wood rested on the floor beside it.

Off in the corner sat a lamp; it was the only lighting in the entire room, but it was dim. I could barely see it. Squinting my eyes while I stared at it more deeply, I noticed it wasn't a lamp at all. It was an oil-burning lantern. The flicker of the light leisurely jumped while the shadows danced across the wall.

My eyes darted off to the other side of the room when bam, it felt like someone slapped my thoughts with a bat.

"Oh my God! I'm sitting on top of Chip! He's right here, and he's not dead!"

"He's not dead!" I repeated it silently, "I made it all up!"

Excitement took over, almost near explosion, when I lowered my eyes and saw his head buried against my bosom.

"Is this real?" I asked myself.

My hands became the immediate focus. I needed to make sure I could really feel him. I could. "Did I make up his murder inside my head? Did I imagine, all this time, that he died when he didn't?"

Accepting that I made everything up, I paused my racing thoughts and came to a quick conclusion. Yes, I only dreamed Chip was murdered.

"Oh, thank you, Jesus! He didn't die! I made it all up!"

My eyes tightly closed, I savored the sensation of his body under mine. My heart was beating fast as I squeezed him tighter and tighter with my legs, feeling his warmth against my skin. "Ah yes, I can feel him. I can really feel him."

His body, his energy, his warmth—he felt so good. "Why did I imagine such a brutal death for him?" I tortured myself. "What the hell was I thinking?"

Unlocking my eyes, I sneaked a peek at his head again.

"No, he didn't die. Everything I thought real was just a horrible nightmare. Chip's right here, right this second, he's right here."

I took in a deep breath and tried to relax as I released it.

"I feel like I've missed him terribly. Why is that?"

The surrender was powerful. The sensation of his body against me was overwhelming. I wanted to stay in that exact moment forever, never allowing him to get away again. Wrapping my arms around his head, I held him tightly. Happiness sprinkled inside of me while I tenderly rocked us back and forth, ever so slowly.

Out of nowhere, a loud voice exploded from my chest. "You're bleeding! You need to go and clean up."

Instant panic devoured me. There was no time to think when I jumped up as fast as I could and stood in front of Chip. Confusion set in instantly. Why did he say that?

I glanced down at my legs and searched for the sight of blood, but there was none. I looked over at Chip searching his lap, but there was nothing on him either. Yet, his tone, it highly suggested it.

I couldn't help but wonder, "Am I on my period?"

Chip didn't like the sight of blood, I knew that. Even if he was a medic in the Navy, he didn't care for it. I would never put him in this predicament. Why in the world have I done this now?

It was an embarrassing moment, one where I couldn't find words to express anything. I stood in silence, rummaging through mixed up thoughts. Chip stood up and stared hard into my eyes, saying nothing.

Slowly, he turned to his right and walked away. I stared at his naked body until he disappeared into the bedroom ahead.

I felt a quick inkling of dejection from his reaction, but the nosy in me was curious, too. All of my attention was thrown back to the brilliant green couch and the blood comment simply vanished.

"This room isn't familiar," I whispered. "It doesn't feel like home; where are we? What is this place and why are we here?"

It wasn't pretty at all.

The room seemed old and the smell was God-awful. The ancient scent reminded me of musty, moldy, moth balls. I was starting to feel ill, and very creeped out, too.

There was no other furniture in the room. The distant oil lantern seemed to be sitting on top of a dark table, and the shaggy carpet was matted from obvious travel. A pathway could be seen leading from the couch straight to the fireplace, and another trail led to a room off to my left.

"Why on earth are we in this dump?" I cried out.

Unexpectedly, a bright light emerged from a faraway kitchen. Amidst the light, I saw a table in another area, a dining room maybe. My curiosity, of course, beckoned. So secretly and very quietly, I commenced to move toward the brightness of the other room.

I tiptoed, looking back every other step to make sure I was still alone. One foot up, gently I placed it onto the floor; next foot up, it too was quietly placed in front of the last. The curiosity in me was in full swing, but I didn't want Chip to catch me; he always told me I was too nosy. I always disagreed and yet, there I was doing exactly what he accused me of—

snooping.

After sneaking past a small corner, the kitchen became more visible. Like a cat on the hunt, I stealthily moved a bit faster when I noticed a small table butted up against the wall to my right. With it, were four chairs. One was set up at each corner while the other two faced a set of pantry doors that were located to my left. The dining room was tiny; maybe the size of a small hallway.

My focus remained on the kitchen, so I proceeded past the table. With every second step forward, I stopped to look back. Chip hadn't appeared yet, and I kept creeping ahead knowing that if he caught me, all hell would break loose.

The closer I got, the brighter the kitchen appeared. The floor was vividly white and I could see a long, immaculate, countertop sitting far off in the distance, too. It reminded of Mr. Clean's kitchen, like the one in the commercial. White cabinet doors sparkled while the entire room permeated cleanliness.

When I reached the second chair, the one facing the pantry doors, a very loud noise was heard. It was a very disturbing rattling sound and one that made me stop dead in my tracks. While I attempted to grasp my new reality, I turned to face the skinny doors.

"Okay," I whispered. "The doors are shaking."

I was beyond bewildered. Completely still, I stared hard. There were two white pantry doors—they looked like thin shutters—and each one had a small white handle.

"Why are they shaking so badly?" I questioned.

I looked up; the doors reached the ceiling. I looked down; they touched the floor. Unexpectedly, the severity of the shaking became louder; it was relentless. Behind me I could feel the table and chairs bouncing against the wooden floor. It had gotten worse, if that was possible.

"Apparently, someone is stuck inside," I resolved out loud. "Should I open the door and let them out?"

Well, of course I should!

I took one step closer and slowly raised my hand forward. Prepared for what may come, I placed my hand on the knob and situated my feet to pull the door open.

"But what if I'm attacked?" I questioned. "What if I can't get away?"

I had somehow walked into a horror flick and was now aware that there was a possibility the outcome may not go as planned. So I removed my hand and took one step back. Standing in place, I waited for the disturbing scene to end.

Several minutes passed. The shaking was worse and the noise was earth shattering louder. The doors were rocking so hard, I feared them falling from their hinges. Keeping a straight head was difficult and thinking logically was a loss cause. Whoever stood behind those doors wanted out badly.

"What is it I'm so scared of?" I asked myself.

Opening them and letting the person out was the right thing to do. I knew that. Doing nothing wasn't going to change anything.

"If I don't help, they'll remain there inside," I convinced myself. "Why would someone be locked up inside of a pantry to begin with?"

I took one step closer, placed my right hand on the small handle once again, and pulled it open very slowly.

In a flash, a white smoky something crashed through the doors. It speedily rushed out, raced, and smashed right inside of me. My whole body jerked, my arms flew out, and my knees buckled. I had lost control of everything.

The impact riddled me with expansive turmoil.

My balance was gone as I stumbled back a few steps. My breathing skipped a beat as I gasped hard for a breath of air. My hands slammed hard into my chest pressing firmly against my heart. Every thought had vanished. I rocked with sudden confusion.

Ah, now I remember.

It became imperative I assess my situation, so I lifted my heavy hands to study, turning them over twice. I searched for any clue or sign of trouble, but nothing out of the ordinary was noticed. I hadn't been hurt and wasn't in any kind of pain.

*One thing was certain. This thing was **not** Chip.*

"So who is it then? Why have I been possessed?" I questioned myself. "Wait a minute... is Chip dead?"

Confusion was setting in again.

"Have I been possessed?"

My eyes darted straight ahead and looked up, back at the white, now swinging... pantry doors.

"I must scream for help!"

The next thing I know...

I'm back in that old living room, standing in front of Chip. He's sitting on the green couch, looking up at me. When his eyes met mine, I felt the intense power of his stare.

"What's he trying to tell me?"

Oftentimes, I understood his expressions, but right now, not so much. As a matter of fact, I didn't feel anything from him, or from me, for that matter. I did, however, recognize the commanding silence.

Out of nowhere, my skin started to crawl. My throat was swelling and I couldn't swallow. I raised my hands to my neck and massaged it; it was protruding and growing larger and larger by the second. As fast as I could, I rubbed my hands up and down like a wild man, trying to make it stop. Fear had profoundly now, kicked in.

"Why am I losing control of my body?"

"Oh wait!" I screamed. "What's this? Am I freaking floating?" I was always a sucker for an adrenaline rush.

It was so invigorating! And much more intriguing than my rapidly expanding body. A great urge to explore came over me, so I tried to look below at the floor.

My neck had grown so large that it wouldn't bend. It was difficult to move anything really, but with all of my might, I forced myself to lean forward and stretched my head out as far as I could. The attempt had me feeling ill, almost to the point of vomiting, but I changed my focus and searched for my feet.

Finally, success. My eyes shifted to glance at the floor and yes, I was indeed floating all of three feet from the ground. This threw me into exhilaration. I felt like a child again. I was so happy that little droplets of tears seeped from my eyes.

"I'm flying, I'm flying," I shouted. "Holy crap, look at me, Chip. I'm flying!"

Staring directly into his eyes, I repeated it over and over again. His smile was inviting; he looked so happy for me. But it was all short lived. The happiness faded when I noticed something strange that took me my surprise.

My voice had gotten deeper and deeper in tone. It was no longer mine. Whatever it was in that closet earlier, was without a doubt still inside of me. It had officially taken over my body and now my voice, too.

Without warning, I was grabbed up, pulled out, and thrown to the side of the couch. I had been ripped from my body and was now a bystander with a front row seat. I could see everything. My deep voice was still saying, I'm flying, but it was nothing but a big lie. My body wasn't flying, it was floating, right smack dab in front of Chip.

I watched as my abducted body made a fist and pointed its index finger to the floor. It had turned into a very rude, ugly Being, and was demanding, not asking, but demanding Chip's undivided attention. When I heard the loud curdling scream it possessed, a wave of shock charged right through me.

"Get over here," it hollered, "right now!"

Chip didn't move. He sat in place staring up at my unrecognizable face. His eyes were large and very inquisitive. The insistent behavior of this thing didn't give up as it continued to demand his affection. Accepting no for an answer wasn't an option.

"Are you not listening to me?" it yelled.

All I could do was observe all of the weirdness as I bounced back and forth between the two. But then I heard a loud screech that jolted me into submission. It was thunderous, to the point where the whole world would have heard it. I jerked in complete fright.

"I told you to get over here," it screamed, "right now!"

My eyes bolted open and my heart was racing out of control. My fingers were tightly grasping the covers and my breathing was so fierce, that all I could hear was my heartbeat beating loudly inside of my head.

Thump thump, thump thump, thump thump...

And then it struck me— it was an outrageous dream.

I couldn't help it though. I examined every corner of my room. That dream was so real, it had me searching hard for the white ghostly Being and at the same time, I prayed to God I didn't find one.

"I'm okay. I'm *safe* here in my bed," I chanted, "I'm okay." I sat up and glared into the darkness of the walls. My heartbeat subsided, but the chill of fear remained. I lifted my arm to my head and wiped it clean of the sweat from my brow.

In the dim blue glow from my clock, I looked at my hands again. I checked my legs and my feet, too, to make sure everything was still okay.

My thoughts were increasingly louder as well, and asking a ton of questions. *Do I need to be worried? Do I need to be more careful? Do I need to cleanse my house of spirit activity?*

"Is this thing still inside of me?" I yelled, hoping for an answer. I seriously needed to talk to Chip.

And then I shouted at the top of my lungs, hearing its echo glide through the house.

"What the hell was that about, Chip?"

Chapter Three

Presents

S till frightened and sitting straight up in bed, I forced my mind to stay calm while my speeding heart raced wildly. Staying focused on being as still as possible seemed important, but the haunting silence of the room embraced me, wrapping its dark arms tightly around my shoulders. My thoughts however, took immediate flight.

"Am I going crazy? Was that as *real* as it felt?"

I had no idea if I was okay or not.

Folding my pillow behind me, I scooted back and stared into the glowing dark. I couldn't do anything else and I couldn't budge another inch. I just stared, hard, at every crack and every shadow that seemed to bounce off the walls.

If that thing, that ghostly Being, was still inside of me—I seriously thought it was—then I wanted to be alert and wide awake to deal with it when it came out.

"Where are you, Chip, when I need you?" I questioned him, but he didn't answer. Even if he did, I doubt I would've heard him. The loud drumming sound of blood rushing through my head was much louder than any flowing thought.

Every so often I turned to look at the clock. I waited for time to painstakingly tick by. An hour passed when I found myself fighting the urge to sleep again. I needed to stay awake because I had to be able to confront the ghostly Being, but my eyes were feeling very, very heavy. I fought it, hard, but I soon lost the battle. I succumbed ...

My back was leaning up against a chair; I felt the firmness behind me. My head was lowered toward my lap and I was sitting straight up with my eyes obviously closed. Ruffling noises could be heard only feet away.

"Ruffling noises?" I silently questioned.

It was a definite sound of paper being wadded. As I became more aware, expertly listening, little by little I lifted my head to see where the sound was coming from.

"Oh my God, there's Chip!" I shouted to myself.

There he was, sitting on the floor across from me. His head was looking down at something in his lap. His arms were moving all around, flailing about. His voice was traveling fast; he was talking up a storm, laughing loudly. I couldn't help but giggle because he was having such a good time. And that laugh of his, oh my gosh, it was fantastically infectious.

I fell captive quickly. I started laughing with him. The magic of joy was spinning all around inside and it lifted me higher than I had been in a very, very long time.

I glanced down at his lap.

"Wow," I was taken aback. "He's wrapping gifts and he's wrapping a lot of them."

There were tons of presents scattered all around him; they were strewn everywhere. Inside of his hands, he was fumbling with a small box. His big fingers weren't allowing him to wrap its tiny size, but he wasn't giving up. Chip was having the time of his life and I was thoroughly amused. It was no secret—Chip loved the Christmas holiday.

His legs were crossed Indian style, which was sort of odd. Chip was a bigger built man and had problems with his knees. I was surprised he was so comfortable sitting that way since I couldn't recall him ever doing that before.

"And where did he find that red checkered flannel shirt?"

The shirt was bright, ghastly loud. I knew he loved bright colors, but not the color red. His hair was a complete mess, totally disheveled. He must have gotten directly out of bed and landed on the floor to wrap.

"Gosh, he's so cute," I said to self. "I wonder what time he got up this morning? To be here alone, wrapping all these gifts, and not comb his hair? What's he up to?"

I glanced over at the coffee table behind him and sitting there, plain as day, was his maroon Starbucks coffee mug. This was the mug he had in his hand when he was shot.

"And he's already made coffee, too? Hmmm..." I scratched my head in thought.

As I gazed back at Chip, a new sensation suddenly dashed through me and I tried to discern the unique rush. "Wow, this feeling—it feels really, really good."

"Being here next to him, it's amazingly peaceful."

"I feel good. I know I'm where I need to be, right here with him. To be this in love with him? To adore him as I do? To understand how complete I feel at this very moment? I'm so lost inside of his love—how does that happen? How on earth does he fill me with so much love?"

I sipped my coffee and stared over the rim. Chip's persistence was warranted, but his style of gift wrapping lacked some fundamental attractiveness. He leaned forward to reach for tape when my hypnotic sensation was interrupted. I decided to take a quick look around the room.

There was wrapping paper everywhere. It was on the couch, on the chairs, on the ottoman, even on the coffee tables. Everywhere I looked, I saw wrapping paper in all kinds of patterns. What a colorful mess. I knew then it would take us hours to clean it up.

"You really like wrapping presents, don't you?" I asked as I turned to watch him again.

"Ab—so—lute—ly!" he excitedly replied.

I had this sinking feeling we were going to be there for a very long while, so I decided to help him. I bounced over to sit beside him.

"It's June, isn't it?" I asked him.

"Why, yes," he said. "Yes, it is."

I didn't know where it came from, but I suddenly had a fantastic idea. I didn't want him to say no, so I sat for a minute figuring out a way to deliver it. In a very sweet, naïve way, I planned my words tactfully. I fidgeted with my task and then gently, slipped it in.

"Sweetie pie, you know what we could do?" He hadn't looked at me yet, but I could see him perfectly in my peripheral vision as I watched his lips move.

"What's that?" he asked.

I lifted my arms and whirled them all around. I was so darn excited because I knew I'd come up with the best idea ever. He'd think it was great too, I just knew he would. Anxiously, I commenced to share.

"Well, we should go shopping and buy everyone's Christmas gifts right now. And then, when we get home you can wrap them. This way, we won't have to worry about shopping when December gets here."

Without warning, none whatsoever, Chip's laughter filled the entire room. He was so loud it literally disturbed me and

46

took me completely off track. I couldn't understand why he was laughing, and laughing so loudly at that. Why would he do that to me again? Did I say something outlandish? Was my idea ridiculous? I didn't think it was all that funny.

I became very frustrated.

He finally stopped chuckling when a big smile stretched across his handsome face, almost to say I'm sorry, but I wasn't buying it. I knew he was snickering at me again, so I sat there, waiting to hear what he had to say for himself.

"Let's wait and see what happens, okay?" he said.

Oh no he didn't! Why that same old line again? Why? I heard that very response a million times before and I hated it with a passion. He never gave me a straight answer, ever. It was so easy to say "yes" or "no," but with Chip, everything was such a difficult decision-making process. That was the one thing that irritated me most about him.

I leaned my head back and closed my eyes for a minute. I was very frustrated, yet I didn't want him to see my disappointment. We're not on the same page, that's all. I took a deep breath and only then, did I open my eyes.

We were standing in front of the stove. He was leaning against me while we poured chili from one container into another, and then sealed them up tight.

I silently questioned our madness, but just as I did, his voice grabbed a hold of me. His gentle tone vibrated through my ears while he rambled in conversation. I could hear us talking, but I couldn't quite grab its grip yet. Not until he said this ...

"Check the cupboard above for more cans of chili, love."

I reached up and opened the white cabinet door, but all that was there were our Tupperware bowls and a couple of cans of soup.

"I only see two chicken noodle soups, sweetie. We don't have any more chili," I told him, as I continued to study the contents.

"We'll have to get more later," he whispered.

I then took a few steps back and positioned myself behind Chip as I watched him seal the last containers. "Do you want me to fix us something to eat?" I asked him.

"No, not yet," he took several seconds to respond. He closed the last lid, turned slightly to the left and swiped his hands twice—as to say I'm all done.

He then turned completely around and faced me. My cheeks rose slowly as my mouth formed a perfect smile. His eyes sunk into mine when I noticed the expression on his face; soft and full of life.

Chip's eyes—the most brilliant, beautiful, ocean blue eyes I'd ever seen—were hypnotic. I was submerged into his trance, but was able to recognize that smile, it matched his baby blues. He was happy.

After picking up my hand and wrapping it into his, he nodded, oh so slightly, and then gently guided me into the living room. Seconds later, we were entering a very long hallway, a hallway I didn't recognize.

I had no idea where I was and could feel my instant reservation. Stopping in my tracks, I stared down the white, empty, tubular gateway. I could see that it lead to a different living room but not to one I was familiar with. Not knowing where he was taking me filled me with uneasiness, yet at the same time, I understood there was nothing to worry about as long as he was with me, so I decided not to pull away.

Chip suddenly released my hand and wrapped his arm around my waist. We walked down a never-ending hallway via a very slow stroll toward a never-reaching living room. His hand was rubbing across my behind, a sign of comfort for me, a sign of his love for me, and this helped me feel less anxious. I leaned my head back into his shoulder and looked up into his face. Unexpectedly, his head was diving toward mine and I closed my eyes to wait.

His soft lips pressed firmly against my forehead. I acknowledge his sweet kiss and pushed myself further into his shoulder when his body began to wiggle. I felt his face still next to mine and knew his lips were very close to my ear. And then he whispered... ever so slowly.

"D-o y-o-u c-u-m?"

My thoughts shot through the roof. Instantly, I was thrown into a tizzy. Why did he ask me that? Irritation creeped in, a little bit, when I found myself wanting to lash out, "Darn it, Chip, you know better!" But I didn't say a word. I feared if I said anything, or told him what I was thinking, I'd only hurt his feelings. We had come such a long way in our relationship, I couldn't bear the thought of saying something that could potentially jeopardize our progress.

Facing each other in the middle of the hallway now, he grabbed me with his magnetic stare; it was obvious he enjoyed doing that. But sometimes he made me uncomfortable with it. On occasion, it felt like he could see right through me and quite possibly, speak directly to my soul. There were things in my past I didn't want him to know.

"He seriously wants me to answer that crazy question, doesn't he?" There wasn't a doubt he was waiting for me to respond and in turn, I was waiting for him to change the subject. But time felt like it was dragging on forever.

"Seriously?" I hated when Chip did stuff like this. Stomping my foot in wonder, I had to ask myself, "Is he talking about sex?" In an instant, I was taken back in time.

One afternoon, we went for lunch at Cracker Barrel. After being seated, I began to point out some of the old artifacts that caught my eye. Chip was seated across from me when I noticed him leaning across the table, heading toward me. I had a glass of tea in my hand and was raising it up to take a drink. At the same time, I had turned to see what he was up to.

His face was planted directly in front of mine. He was so close he had taken me by surprise. His smile looked different and his eyes—he was on a seek-and-find operation. Acting like he hadn't shocked me, I leaned back to take a sip of tea when his voice slapped me with a whisper.

"Do you think we have sex, or do you think we make love?"

It all happened so fast. I never had a chance to swallow my tea and instead, my first instinct was to scream out loud, "Whhhhhaaaaatttttt?" I choked as "what" exploded from my mouth and the tea, well, the tea splashed out all over his nice shirt.

Repeatedly, I apologized and made every effort to clean him up. Luckily, he thought it was funny and laughed the whole thing off. A few minutes later though, it was obvious how much he wanted an answer to that crazy question.

He said, "Well, what do you think?"

Neither of us were budging, which was typical Chip and Lyn mentality. "He's got to know he shouldn't ask me such a question like that. This is crazy!" Yet, I sensed we weren't going anywhere until I said something. Determined to keep it as simple as possible, I looked up into his eyes and simply said, "Of course."

The biggest smile appeared on his face.

He lit up like a Christmas tree. He grabbed my hand again and this time, wrapped my arm around his and pulled me, encouraging me to continue our walk. All of my thoughts were turning to mush because he was giving me his special, sexy, like you can't resist me, charmed look. I knew he wanted to play, but I wanted to go and freshen up first.

When I looked at the bathroom ahead of us, he released my hand. The weight of his hands rested on top of my shoulders as he glided behind me and slowly exited into that new living room. Somehow, I knew he'd be waiting for me there when I returned.

His smile was gorgeous, almost captivating, as I watched him take a few steps backward. The room he was stepping into was enormous. "Wow, is this our new house?" I wondered. I turned back around and now, I was standing in front of a doorway... to a bathroom. But I wasn't alone.

A young boy was washing his hands at the sink—staring directly at me and smiling. Quite surprised, I questioned how we knew each other since he seemed very excited to see me. His lips were moving, but I couldn't discern his voice. My thoughts were too busy trying to figure out who he was.

Instead of asking him, I rapidly changed my focus to hurry and get back to Chip. I decided to leave the boy and search for the next bathroom. As I walked through my bedroom and marched to the next bathroom, I couldn't help but worry. "Where have I seen that boy before?" I couldn't place him.

I searched for a wash cloth at the sink but couldn't find one. "Whoa, this bathroom has a double vanity. When did I get that?" I asked out loud. "And the counter top is white? But mine's soft beige. I'm confused."

After checking the cabinets and finding no linens, I decided to potty. "When I'm done, I'll head right back to Chip," I said. But once I sat down, I got the surprise of my life.

My eyes were doused with radiant beauty. "Oh my God,

this bathroom reeks of elegance," I was enthralled.

*"I have never in my life seen anything so beautiful—
particularly in a bathroom."*

*The walls were covered in large porcelain stone tiles, all
at least four feet by four feet each and each one separated from
the other in different colors of bright pink, beautiful deep dark
purple, soft cream, rich burgundy, and stunning, stunning gold.
They were absolutely gorgeous.*

*To the right, a beautiful Angel was resting in the middle of
a stone fountain. She looked antique, eggshell white in color,
and her hand was lifted so that her baby soft face rested gently
upon her palm. I watched in awe as the water slowly flowed
from her outstretched wings and saw every color of the
rainbow radiate around her body. She was very pretty.*

*I suddenly gasped for air; I had been holding my breath
for quite some time. Unexpectedly, I saw that the Angel was
sitting between a shower and the largest bathtub ever made. I
looked down at the floor and followed the garden stones
leading up to the shower. There were no doors attached.*

*Instead, it had Victorian style drapery hanging from the
ceiling at its entrance, welcoming the occupant. The walls were
covered in decorated rock and there were golden bars leading
into the shower that shined brightly, each one displaying little
white, sparkling, stars.*

*On the other side of the Angel fountain was a mammoth-
sized circular stone bathtub. The golden oak color was
mesmerizing with bits of white streaks cascading throughout. I
was captivated.*

"Holy cow, what is this place?" I blurted.

*At that point, all I could do was soak it in. My eyes danced
across the floor again, staring at gold planter-like ornaments
overflowing with colorful, fanciful, flowers. Hanging from the*

ceiling were spectacular peach, white, and yellow flowers while on the floor, golden arched hanging planters stuffed with green foliage draped the elegant tiles.

"I'm in heaven. I have to be in heaven," I shouted. "There's no place like this that can possibly exist. There can't be." When I turned my head to the left, the largest Jacuzzi ever, stole my eyes; it was gigantic.

"Oh, this must be a Queen's bathroom," I hollered. "This is so rich." Oblivious to everything, I had officially been kidnapped from the outside world.

Unexpectedly, the bathroom door swung open.

Reality punched me hard as I gasped for air again. Someone had startled me. When I turned to look, I saw the same little boy I ran into earlier. He hadn't knocked, he didn't announce himself— he just barged right through the door while I sat embarrassingly on the toilet.

He was talking, bantering on and on about something, but he had scared and humiliated me so badly, I couldn't register a single word he was saying. Instead, I raised my hand into the air to suggest his silence.

"Please give me my privacy," I requested.

He spoke no more. His head lowered to the floor. The disappointment was written all over his small, innocent face, but I said nothing else. With his little shoulders drooping, he gradually turned around and slowly walked out.

My heart was broken. I was crushed. I knew I had hurt his feelings. And then a redirect rushed in, "I must get back to Chip!" I quickly started searching for the toilet paper and just as I located it, Chip's mom walked in.

Instantly, I became a little edgy.

"Why can't I have a little bit of privacy?" I pondered.

Like the small boy, she started talking, too. Once again I

heard nothing because my thoughts were somewhere else—it's all I could think about—I need to get back to Chip. He's waiting for me.

I wanted her to stop talking even while I sensed her urgency to discuss something. But then she hopped up onto the counter, scooted her butt back and dangled her legs over the edge. Oh God, she's staying.

"Can she not see I want to take care of my business in private and get back to Chip? Do I do this in front of her and then excuse myself and walk out? Or do I sit here and wait, wait for her to understand that I'm patiently waiting for her to leave."

All of a sudden, my hand began to ache. The pain was strong and I shook it hard to wake it up. As I swung it back and forth vigorously, I accidentally hit it against the marble toilet paper holder.

"Wow, that should've hurt," I said, out loud. But it didn't.

As I continued my efforts to bring my hand back to life, I suddenly realized I wasn't sitting on a toilet anymore. I was somewhere else.

I recognized his scent immediately. Although my eyes were closed and I could see nothing but dark, I knew Chip was on top of me, hugging me tightly.

"I love you, Lynnie," he whispered.

The sound of his voice danced in from everywhere. It wasn't just entering my ears, it came in as waves of love that flowed through my body all at once.

Each wave carried with it an intense erotic sensation and quickly, they began to take over. I had never felt such strong, pulsating, arousing, stabs like these ever before. I couldn't help but moan with pleasure.

He hadn't even touched me yet and I was unexplainably

turned on.

Picking me up, Chip placed me underneath him. As he spread my legs apart, wrapping them around his back, I felt his face lean close to mine. His hands gently ran through my hair and then he whispered again, "Do you want more?"

This time, I welcomed his question. Unlike before, the words danced around my head in a circle and without warning, quickly leaped into my essence through the top of my head. As I felt the entrance of their electricity, my whole body jerked in pleasure and once again, his voice filled me with chills of an indescribable stimulation. From the tips of my hair to the tips of my toes, I was indeed aroused and yearning for him.

Slowly, and very gently, he guided himself inside of me. In an instant, my body went limp and fell backwards. My world consisted of pure sensations and my entire Being rocked in waves of ecstasy.

I wanted him, all of him; I loved making love to him.

Suddenly, I became aware of how weightless I felt. I couldn't feel my head, or my chest, or my legs for that matter. And something else was happening, too. Even though we were intertwined, we were also moving, floating, flying in circles, rotating, somewhere.

And then, Chip pulled me closer and tighter, thrusting, moving in time, and I knew I wouldn't last long; I could feel it boiling inside. Moments later, the strongest orgasm washed over me. Fireworks exploded inside my head, my heartbeat was bursting, and every organ inside of me rocked in spastic convulsions.

I was encompassed in an orgasmic realm of blissful pleasure.

My eyes finally opened when what I saw before me, was nothing short of a miracle. Everything was black, but it was the most beautiful darkness I had ever seen. Bright stars were rushing by, galaxies of vibrant colors, shapes, and sizes, were everywhere gliding through space. Wrapped soundly around Chip and I, was a beautiful, iridescent, color of blue and I knew instantly it was an aura surrounding us.

Us... we wore no body. We were of the soul and were complete and divine energy. Although I could still feel him embracing me, physically, I also knew we constructed this through our thoughts. We were intelligent and loving Beings, able to create whatever we wanted, whenever we wanted, through the Love that we carried within.

Unbound by our bodies, unbound by the limits of my human thoughts, and upon the opening of my eyes, it was unveiled ... we are powerful Beings of Light.

In our Infinite Wisdom, we knew everything.

All of a sudden, I wasn't floating in space anymore. Instead, I was lying in bed. In no time flat, I knew what had happened.

"Oh wow," my voice bounced through the air. "Did we just make love in outer space?"

The idea of something like that happening was unfathomable. But I had to admit, everything inside of me was still tingling. It was true. We had sex somewhere out there in that big Universe. Wow.

I jumped out of bed and headed to the kitchen for coffee. I knew there wasn't a chance in hell anyone would believe me if I told them my dead fiancé made sweet love to me.

"Chip's still alive. He has to be… that was too real!"

Chapter Four

Skeptical Me
with Megan Riley

S omething wasn't right. My dream life *was* more real and this physical life felt like the dream. I knew that didn't make good sense, but it seriously felt like the truth.

The image of that ghostly Being slamming into my body confused the heck out of me. I asked myself time and again if it really happened. I couldn't help it. This didn't seem normal and questioning my sanity with a fine-tooth comb was all I could do.

The following day, I heard these words escape me. "Why am I dreaming of my dead fiancé like he's still alive?" I certainly marveled at the dreams occurring, but I questioned *everything* about them.

"Are dreams real?" I needed to know for sure. "Or are they a figment of my imagination?" I had the hardest time releasing the skepticism.

Yet, I knew everything I had experienced up to that date was leading me to believe dreams were as real as my physical world. I *knew* they were Chip's way to communicate with me; I had learned that many months ago. But no matter what he did, I always questioned if it was him or if it was me making it all up.

Dealing with the grief and Chip being gone was still very hard. There were many days I huddled in bed, clothes on, reliving his last moments of life, and crying uncontrollably. The sadness remained, hard core, but little by little I found myself focusing more on the signs he delivered. I knew what he was doing. He wanted me to focus on him, and not his murder.

Easier said than done!

To be honest, the *dream-visits* did help. They brought me back to life, a little bit. When I woke from each one, it felt like I had spent the night with the man I love. The magic that consumed me was soothing and the energy I felt from seeing him was glorious and comforting. If euphoria can even tap into the lustrous emotions one can feel from such an experience, then that's the perfect word: euphoria.

I also felt like I had a secret. A big secret that no one in the world would ever believe... the *love of my life* wasn't dead.

It never failed though. Hours later, the marvel would wear off and the questioning ways would set back in. The sadness of his departure would once again weigh heavy on my heart and my depressive nature would take over.

"I've created this madness somehow," I'd tell myself. "This dream life isn't real, the signs I see aren't real, and the songs I hear in my head, they aren't real either. I've created the best fiction movie in the world... or have I?"

How can I imagine something so scary? Why would I create a ghostly Being and make it fly inside of me and then disappear? Why would I create a movie-like dream where Chip is alive, where he's touching me, where he's guiding me, and then ultimately witness a heavenly bathroom? And let us not forget his crazy question he insisted I answer that ultimately lead to an amazing sexual experience out in space. I couldn't make it up even if I tried. I wasn't that good.

It was time to intentionally evaluate my feelings and my health, too. I didn't feel awfully bad. I knew I wasn't *as* depressed as I used to be, but I had to admit it. Taking care of me wasn't a big priority.

I didn't wear make-up anymore. I hadn't gone to the salon in months and I now had a crown of white hair. I was looking older than my years; I could see it. But I didn't care. When Chip died, I remember saying it, *my life isn't ever going to be the same*, and I knew it. I was guilty of living, of surviving, and this was my way to punish myself.

However, over the last weeks, my curiosity was getting the best of me. The new style of *dream delivery* was quite fascinating, even if it was scary. When one feels the actual physicality of doors shaking in front of them, when one experiences the entrance of something inhuman into their body, then one will begin to question the difference between sleep, and awake.

Is there a difference between the two?

I understood the wrapping of Christmas presents and knew this was Chip's way of giving me a gift and telling me how much he loved doing it. But what I didn't get was everything else once we parted ways. Like the beautiful bathroom, the little boy, Chip's mom popping in, and of course, the intense dream about the ghost taking over. It was a bit overwhelming and I became lost in the ability to interpret.

So I decided to turn to the one person who helped me survive his murder. She was my rock in the first months when I sometimes imagined it all unreal—his disappearance.

Shortly after Chip died, I began a search for help in

deciphering the countless dream-visits I had experienced. At the same time, I was very worried about him, too. Not knowing if he was okay, was communicating out of desperation, or was stuck between two worlds—someone told me he was—it was all tearing me up inside. And then I found Megan, a medium out of Colorado.

She was the one person who made my communications with Chip feel positive and real. She helped me understand, above everything else, that life *does* continue past physical death. At a time when I needed major help, big answers, loving guidance, this woman gave me all of that and so much more. She gave me... *Hope.*

"I'm really confused," I told Megan. After sharing the ghost dream, the bathroom, and the little boy dream, and intentionally leaving out the sex in space dream, I added, "The dreams feel more real than this life here. That's not right, is it?"

"Sounds like an odd night of dreams," she said. "The second one (Chip wrapping Christmas presents), he's giving you gifts all the time and he loves it. He loves everything about it; planning and then executing the plan. It's very sweet."

"The kitchen is the heart you know, the nourishment of the home and of us. Chip still provides you nourishment. The bathroom is vulnerable, especially when we're sitting there. You felt strong enough to tell the little boy to give you privacy, but not his mom. You may feel she is blocking you from Chip and from experiencing him. You may feel you have no privacy with her and that she's unconscious to your concerns about this."

"Okay," I responded. "That makes sense. What do you think the beautiful bathroom might have meant?"

"The bathroom is also the internal," she said. "You've had so many dreams with the bathroom. I think the beauty of the bathroom is what Chip represents—beauty and the sense of abundance."

"And the little boy?" I asked. "Could that be Chip's brother?"

In our first medium reading, Megan and I learned that when Chip crossed, a little boy had held his hand. Later, we also learned the young boy was Chip's brother.

"The little boy could be his brother that he brings along," Megan replied. "Especially since the first bathroom you went into he was there and you didn't think anything of it. And that he listened to you when you asked him to leave from the second bathroom. They are together now, and that would make sense."

"I'm scared to ask, but what did you think about that ghost dream?" I wasn't convinced I *really* wanted to know.

"Whoa! That one feels like a fear that you're going to lose yourself again, in a man or in a relationship or just while life happens; being invisible while not being you. Being taken over while not listening to yourself and needing someone else to tell you what's going on. Thinking that it will never be as good as it was."

"I don't see that happening to you or for you," she continued. "You know what feels right and wrong and you are hearing the silence in yourself and your body. Does that resonate?"

Does that resonate? Heck yeah, it did. It was complete confirmation when she said his presents were gifts; I knew that. And when she said he was enjoying the planning, a state of bliss blanketed me.

It was very interesting to also learn that the kitchen and the bathroom symbolized so much, spiritually speaking. The kitchen provided nourishment and the bathroom symbolized both vulnerability and the internal self. Chip seriously loved the bathroom. It didn't matter if he was sitting on the toilet or taking a shower, he was always taking me to the bathroom in dreams.

As for his mom, I understood that, too. Unconsciously, I must have worried if she understood my love for her son. If anyone knew the love and connection they had together, I certainly did. I had watched this once vibrant woman completely crumble to pieces after his murder. I witnessed her pain, her sorrow, and her depression as it consumed her. I saw a mother fight like hell to survive her son's death.

Yes, I knew firsthand her love for Chip. And I knew Chip's love for his mom, too. What I wanted to believe was that *our* love for him would outweigh everything that was happening, or would happen in the future, and that alone would keep us close to who we both knew him to be.

The ghost dream—oh yeah I was taken over. Even my voice changed into someone I didn't recognize. And maybe it was a fear. I've had lots of fears since Chip died. I've also tried extremely hard to remain open and positive. Did I think I was going to get lost in life and not live my purpose?

I had no way of knowing for sure. It would certainly depend on the choices I made or the path I was to follow. I knew I could pretend the *afterlife communications* were a fluke and gradually sink back into the blinded society I came from. That was certainly an option, but not an option I believed Chip would allow me to accept very easily.

Chip trampled his way into a girl whose future may have been undecided, but was one of complete confidence in her recent years of independence. She was also a girl who didn't want her newfound confidence taken away, ever again.

The only thing I wanted from Chip was for him to love

me. Not to love me for what I could do for him or for what I could give him, or vice versa, but to sincerely love each other for who we were. It didn't matter how much money we had or didn't have; I didn't even care where we lived because nothing else mattered as long as we were happy... and he loved me for me.

Visiting these last few words, *he loved me for me*, reminded me of the day before he died.

Chapter Five

The Day Before

Tuesday, January 22, 2008

Our four month old Lab, Scooby, had a scheduled vet appointment for his next set of shots on Tuesday, the twenty-second. Our appointment was at three o'clock and Chip was already home taking care of the kids while I rushed around to leave work early.

The best I could do was one o'clock. After parking the car and heading up to the front door, I figured I'd hear the dogs barking frantically waiting to greet me.

Surprisingly, there was nothing. All I heard was complete silence. I opened the door thinking they'd be outside, but I was in for a shocker. They weren't outside. Instead, they were living it up luxury style.

What a sight to behold. Against the wall in the living-room sat our long, deep cherry leather couch. All three of them—Chip, Angel, and Scooby—were sitting on it together. Chip's long legs were stretched out in front of him resting on top of the coffee table; he was watching the television. Angel, our thirteen year-old Chihuahua, was lying in his lap, comfortably sleeping. And Scooby, dear ole Scooby, was sprawled out on top of the cushions, resting his left paw on top of his daddy's shoulder.

Chip had the kids relaxing, peacefully. How he kept those two so calm always amazed me and what a perfect Kodak moment it was. The picture was pure joy.

That peaceful moment vanished immediately when they saw me at the door. The kids leaped off the couch and ran to greet me. I knelt down to play and say my hellos and receive my happy whines and slobbery kisses. Amidst my happy lovin', I looked over at Chip's beaming grin.

His smile briefly hypnotized me until I was drawn to his hand covered in little red, dripping dots. I released myself from the clutches of the kids and walked over to sit beside him, seeing the new scratches on his arm too. *Poor Chip.* It literally looked like a cat had him for lunch. I took his hand into mine and turned it over to observe how badly he'd been attacked.

"I was rough housin' with Scoob," he said. "But I think he got the better of me." He held out his other hand for me to examine, as well. "Those damn teeth of his. They're still sharp as needles."

We laughed, but when I observed more closely, a deep cut appeared on the tip of his finger. Scooby attacked him good and he was still bleeding. I hopped up and went to the bathroom to grab the peroxide and a Band-Aid.

Chip had been pretty sick the previous couple of days and his coloring was still very pale. I bandaged up his boo-boo and then turned to meet his eyes. "Sweetie. Why don't you go and lie down until it's time to leave? I'll come in and wake you up, okay?"

There was no argument; he was off to bed. I think I was hoping he'd decline, but there I was left with complete boredom for a solid hour and a half. I seriously couldn't wait for it to go by.

At long last, the time had arrived to wake him. I opened the door and heard the low volume of the TV. I unhurriedly walked around the nightstand and gently placed my hand on top of his right arm.

"Chip. It's time to get up," I whispered. But he didn't move. *Now what do I do?*

I'd never had to wake him before because he was always up before me. He told me a story once about waking him from a deep sleep—*don't do it.* If I ever did, he said he couldn't be held responsible for scaring the heck out of me.

I scratched my head, *Well, I don't want to get up there and jump up and down on the bed then, do I?* No, that wouldn't be a very good idea.

"Sweetie pie," I wiggled him tenderly. "It's time to get up."

Nothing, he wasn't moving a muscle. For some peculiar reason, I started wondering if he was faking. I leaned in closer to his face and watched his eyes. I stared intently at each one looking for rapid movements. Why I did this, I don't really know, but I did it. They weren't bouncing; he was definitely asleep. "Okay, one more attempt and that's it," I whispered.

"Chip, wake up," I lightly shook him again. "It's time to take your son to the vet." I was met with the same reaction once again, nothing. I silently exited the bedroom and closed the door behind me. *He needs his rest.*

Man, I didn't want to go and do it alone. Scooby was a big boy and had no problem dragging me around. We had signed him up for obedience training the week before but had attended only one class so far. We still had such a long way to go.

Since Chip wasn't accompanying me, I had to gather my

composure and go with the program. I packed up Scooby's treat bag, leashed him up, and then ran him out to the car. As long as we were inside the car, we were good. He loved poking his head out the back windows letting the fast air wrinkle up his face. We lived only a mile or so from the vet's office.

After putting the car into park, I turned to face Scooby in the back seat. Planted across his big face looked like a huge smile. He was panting up a storm, drool was dripping all over the place, his long tail was whacking against the rear windows... it wasn't a good sign, but I calmly began my speech anyway.

"Okay, boy. It's just you and me here. Don't make me look like a complete fool when we get inside, okay?" I reached in to pet him when our eyes locked for a second. *I wonder if he understands me? Man, I don't want to do this alone.*

We hopped out of the car and walked up to the entrance. So far, so good. Slowly, I opened the door and tugged once on his leash and silently prayed for him to be calm.

Yeah, right. Seconds passed before the realization set in— there was no controlling my sixty-five pound beast. He was off and running. My big monster puppy was literally pulling me across the tile floors—I had forgotten to change my shoes. He was tracking the people sitting quietly and smelling all the behinds in his new arena. We, no—I—must have looked like an absolute fool.

"Darn it, Scooby," I cussed inside. "You're killing me here, dude." I kicked off my sandals to gain traction and pulled him away from the scents. Finally, I was allowed to sign in.

We found a spot just for us when my cell started to ring. The hair on the back of my neck stood straight up; I feared if I let go, Scooby would take off again. But he remained still after I removed one hand and after picking up the phone, Chip's voice surprised me.

"Hey, darlin'. Do you think you might have forgotten something at home?"

I laughed out loud and told him no matter how many times I tried, he wouldn't wake up.

"You could have just put Scooby up in the bed with me," he said. "That would have woke me up."

Now, why didn't I think of that?

"So how did you wake up?" I asked.

"Angel started screaming when you guys left. Her horrible crying woke me. She doesn't like to be left behind, does she?" I had no idea, but obviously not and she let him know it, too.

In a matter of minutes Chip walked through the door. He was so tall and handsome. His eyes located us and a big smile crawled across his face. When Scooby saw his daddy, that was it, he was off to greet dad. There was no hanging on and boy, I was one happy girl. That dog, Chip's little boy, he was too big. And for the moment, he was daddy's problem.

"He's growing at the rate of a Saint Bernard," the doc said. For the second time in a row he told us, "I don't know what you guys are feeding him, but keep it up. He's a healthy young boy."

Looking over at Chip, I saw the incredible beam on his face. He was happy and so proud. Yep, he was the proud daddy of that growing giant dog. Scooby was a cutie, there was no denying that, but I was a bit worried how large he would become. Chip promised he'd take care of him. He promised to spend quality time with him and even take him in his big rig. Ha! I couldn't wait to see that.

We had planned Scooby's upcoming training program and were going all the way. Next Christmas, our day was going to be spent at a Children's Hospital. We wanted to spread love and let Scooby bring a little bit of joy for the holiday, as well. Sharing him with kids who couldn't be home would be a wonderful gift for them, and for us too. It was a good plan and one we already informed our families about. Everyone understood it… we wouldn't be spending Christmas Day with the family.

At last, we were home from the vet. We ate dinner, fed the kids, and then looked at the clock. It was already seven-thirty and time for Chip to leave. Lights out was normally by eight o'clock since four in the morning came very early.

I knew it was coming, the good-bye that is. I saw Chip lean up against the sink, but I stayed focused on staring at the kids eating, thinking he was doing the same. Dreading his darn good-bye, I cringed while I waited for it.

Any minute now, he was going to come up behind me, wrap his arms around my waist, wiggle my hair away from my neck with his face, and kiss me softly on the neck. Then, he would whisper in my ear, *it's time for me to go, baby doll.*

"You don't want me to leave, do you?" he stunned me. That's not at all what I expected. And the significance of his words screamed loudly inside my head. I turned to look into his eyes.

"Of course I don't. We've paid our dues, sweetie pie. I'm ready for us to be a real family now." I was a little stunned at my reply. I'm not usually so direct.

He reached out, grabbed my arm, and pulled me to him. He lifted my head and then kissed me softly on the lips. His eyes drowned into mine and then he said something that surprised me more.

"What would you do without me? You wouldn't have anyone to buy you a new car for your birthday, or buy you new clothes, or buy you nice…"

Right there in his tracks, I stopped him. Without thinking, again, words flew off of my lips.

"Sweetie, you don't have to buy me things. I don't *need* you to buy me things. All I want is for you to love me."

He pulled me even closer, kissed me on the forehead, and hugged me tightly. After wrapping my arms around his back, I rested my head against his chest. His voice suddenly danced through the air and sat there.

"Unconditionally," he whispered.

His arms tightened around me more, almost to the point of taking my breath away. Only seconds whisked by when his voice tapped through my head again.

"I want to buy you nice things, baby doll. It makes me feel good to make you happy. I *want* to be the one to make you happy. I love you, Lynnie."

I needed—*wanted*—to say something back. Once again, he took my breath away. I loved this man more than anyone in the world and now he had placed a tremendously powerful word out there, *unconditionally*.

He had grabbed my heart and was squeezing the life right out of me as I fought the tears verging to emerge. I swallowed my planned words, *you make me happy*, and instead, I caressed his hair. Standing on the tip of my toes, I lifted my face to whisper into his ear.

"I love you, my darlin'," I told him. "Oh, so very much."

All of a sudden, a very heavy weight straddled my upper body. It was him, and he was bearing down on me, hard. In slow motion, we started a path to the floor. Fear of falling and busting my behind, I wrapped my hands tightly around his neck to hold myself up. But it wasn't working. Chip lost his balance and we were going down. His arm stretched out when I heard the refrigerator crash into the counter; *boom*. But not even that stopped us from landing flat on the floor; he was lying on top of me.

All we could do was laugh. We giggled so hard that we hadn't the strength to lift ourselves up. Our stomachs were bouncing with every breath we took. His head popped up from my shoulder and his face flew in front of mine as I closed my eyes tight. When I did, his soft lips caressed my head.

And then we laughed some more.

That afternoon felt like a new beginning for us. It's hard to explain, but on that day I knew we were *forever*. It was obvious we were going to have a wonderful, funny, fantastic life together. Every ounce of my Being told me he was in my life to stay. And even though I experienced these same feelings many, many months earlier, on this day it felt cemented.

My very best friend—was the love of my life.

After Chip's death, I couldn't help but question that word he used, *unconditionally*. *If everything happens for a reason—* was a phrase I often used to start my search for answers. I would start off like this; what if when he said *unconditionally* it spiked the onset of what was to come? What if when he said it, the wheels were put in motion for what inevitably took place less than nine hours later? What if my life is already planned out for me and was for him too? What if when that word passed through his lips, it became his destiny? What if it was his entrance word to go back home? Was that even possible?

Maybe, maybe not.

Is life a designed destiny? Is it already pre-planned before birth? Are there soul agreements, contracts, for each person we meet? Is love the answer? Is everything we experience in life designed to be a lesson in learning the complete emotion of *love*?

Death has an eerie way of finding *unconditional love…*

Chapter Six

Follow the Path

*"The future belongs to those who believe in
the beauty of their dreams." ~Eleanor Roosevelt*

*"O*h Chip, this is gorgeous." *I cried out. "It's so much
prettier here than Florida. We should move here!"*

*Pressed up tightly against the passenger-side window, I
took in the beauty of the coastline. It was simply stunning.*

*"Yeah," I sighed. "We should definitely live here." Chip
stopped the car on the side of the road and we stepped out onto
the grass.*

*He walked around the car and stood behind me, resting his
face on top of my shoulder. Pointing across the waterway
ahead, he announced the little town's name and then gradually
moved to the left as I watched his finger in front of me.*

"And right there, my love," he whispered, "is Tanzania."

*My eyes danced across the crowded neighborhood off in
the distance. Little off-white huts congested the coastline and
unusual lights flickered like stars against the night sky. When I
heard Chip say Tanzania, I focused on one hut because it stood
out above all the rest. It was bright white and at the tip of the
roof, it was shaped into a point. I swore it reminded me of a*

Japanese temple, but I couldn't figure out why it'd be in Tanzania.

Back in the car, Chip driving, I could hear conversation. It was very light-hearted with lots of laughter, but for some odd reason, I couldn't see anything around us. As soon as I questioned my inability to see though, like magic, my physical eyes regained focus. Nothing was clear yet, but I soon figured out why—it was dark of night.

*All of a sudden, I felt sand between my toes. It didn't take a genius to figure out that we were at the beach. It was very murky out but I could hear Chip in front of me; I was following close behind. We were walking toward the ocean and before I knew it, we were strolling **into** the water; I felt the warmth of the sea wrap around my legs.*

"What? Me? Walking into the ocean? Not going to happen!" I said to myself.

But that's exactly what occurred. We were swimming out, bobbing up and down, heading further and further from land. Not yet too far out, I felt Chip's body swim up from behind when his face touched mine. His hand was outstretched in front of us as he pointed to the right.

"Do you see that line there in the water?" he asked. "The colored one that travels next to the buoy?"

"Yes, I do," I responded. "It's there inside the foamy white lines, correct.?"

"Yes. That's where we're going."

He quickly swam around and directly in front of me and then grabbed my hands. He held them firmly, gazing into my eyes and said, "We can never get lost as long as we follow that path."

Why he said something like that, I didn't understand. Because I was barely able to keep up with my surroundings as it was, I focused on my reality... I was in the ocean for Pete's sake.

Off we went, swimming out into the deeper waters.

I'm not an ocean kind of gal and have never liked the thought of being out so far. Ever since the movie, Jaws, I've had no desire to swim in the sea. Just the thought of what lies underneath scares the heck out of me. Yet, there I was, seeming like nothing would harm me, swimming far out into the deepest of waters, totally unafraid. Somehow, I knew I was safe as long as Chip was there with me.

We were talking, laughing, and having a splendid time, when all of a sudden, my attention was torn away and fear rapidly crawled inside. Something other than us made a very, very loud splash. But because it was so dark out, I couldn't see what it was. I leaned over and whispered, "What was that?"

"I don't know," Chip whispered back. "But let's slow down so we don't get in its way."

We immediately stopped paddling our feet and floated in place. And then we waited. And we waited. We waited for this thing to leave so we could keep going. But when I saw an enormous fin rise up and out of the water only inches away, fear kicked in, full speed ahead. I froze. I couldn't move a muscle. I was scared to death and unable to breathe.

When I saw a point at the tip of the fin, that was all it took. Inside somewhere, or maybe I whispered, I couldn't be sure, but I heard me shout—loud and clear, "It's a shark!"

I was petrified, no doubt about it. I was terrified we would be attacked and mangled to pieces. Chip was trying to console me, telling me that everything was going to be okay. A few minutes later, the attention to the big shark had finally been removed. Before I knew it, I heard him say, "All right, let's go."

There was a brilliant glow from the moon upon the water. The large gentle waves had a small bit of white, capping the tips. We floated up to the top, and then down to the bottom. On the crest of one of the them, I decided to get funny and gurgle up some water. Pretending I was having a difficult time staying afloat, I made silly noises. Chip laughed at first, but quickly became stern and reprimanded me.

"Get serious, Lynnie," he said.

As his words hit my ears, an instant awareness of our swimming technique is noticed. We were kicking our feet to move through the water. We weren't using our arms or any other part of our body, just our feet. And nothing was really moving fast, not even us.

*And then out of nowhere, we see **it**.*

***It** was enormous! The largest mammal I'd ever seen, it simply lifted completely out of the water; up, up, high into the air. He was ginormous, creating a solid wall in front of us; it was so close, I knew if I reached my hand out, I could touch him.*

And then he ripplelessly glided down and floated in place, on his side, showing his left flipper. "Is he waving at us?" I wondered. "Isn't that a little odd?"

Even though my heart raced wildly fast with fear, I tried to remain clear-headed and focus on the white circles running through his shiny black skin. His stillness undeniably mesmerized me.

Chip was talking, but not to me. I think he was talking to the mammoth because, in no time it seemed, the whiteness of the circles descended slowly under the water and disappeared.

I was too frightened to move. I wasn't feeling comfortable and just when I thought I was going to stomp my foot and demand to go nowhere else, Chip's comforting voice bounced through my fear.

"Come on, sweetie," he delivered kindly. "It's okay now."

I didn't question him. Instead, I joined him. Off we went again, sliding through the dark sea. The mammoth remained in front, gliding smoothly in and out of the water. He most certainly was a beautiful, magnificent beast.

It took only seconds for my panic to quiet down. As soon as it did, a very clear and concise inner-knowing imprisoned my thoughts; the purpose of the great beast. Intuitively, I knew he was there to lead the way. Something, or someone, told me he was helping us.

"Well, how neat is that?" I whispered. With that thought, with that question, everything instantly changed.

Swimming into a channel of fresh water, two isles could be seen. One was for traffic going in and the other was for traffic leaving. The water was remarkably beautiful, crystal clear in fact, and it felt amazingly warm and tranquil.

Slowly, we swam into the new, beautiful scenery. When I looked over to my right, I marveled at the colors of the water's edge. The green trees, the blue sky above, the yellow and pink flowers dancing in the breeze... it was so beautiful. The water wasn't too deep either; I poked my head in and looked and could see the bottom quite easily. If I wasn't swimming to keep afloat, it'd be difficult for me to believe water was even there. It was that incredibly, crystal clear.

But then something snagged my attention. It was black and moving around underneath me. With no time to process anything, none whatsoever, the object raced to the top, smack in front of me. I had to stop and float in place because there it was, cramming its extra-large nose right in my face.

"Oh my God, is it going to kiss me?" I freaked.

Very puzzled, I started to investigate the nose. It was

massive, round, and very, very wet. I lifted my hand up to reach forward and as soon as I did, the little creature crammed its nose into the palm of my hand. I laughed out loud, loudly. I couldn't help it. Turning quickly toward Chip, I reported my findings.

"It has a round nose. It will not harm us," I shouted. "He's a water cow, sweetie."

"Are you sure about that?" Chip inquired.

"Oh, yes!" I exclaimed, "I'm certain."

I turned back to my new little friend, gently petting him, and softly whispered, "Oh, he's a beautiful baby water cow."

The gentle giant allowed me to pet him a couple more minutes and then slowly he sank into the water and dived out of sight. With that, we set back off to swim. A short distance away a small blockage appeared. We had to climb over it to get to the other side of the isle.

Following behind Chip, he showed me the rocks to step upon. He said he didn't want me to lose my balance and take a tumble. As I stood up to crawl over though, my bathing suit fell from my shoulders. I laughed and said, "Oops, too much water for my top to stay up." We had been in the water for hours, or at least it seemed that way.

I pulled the straps back up and then suddenly recognized the suit I was wearing. It was my black and white swimsuit I had only worn in Hawaii and for the life of me, I couldn't remember getting dressed earlier. Chip was laughing with me as I re-dressed. And then like nothing ever happened, we moved on and climbed over the last set of rocks.

When I raised my head to observe the channel ahead, I gasped deeply for air. Only feet away, sat dozens and dozens of water cows waiting to greet us. They were everywhere and were breathtakingly beautiful. I couldn't move. I stood in *complete awe looking out at the sweet, soft-nosed baby water cows. And then all of a sudden, everything went dark, fast.*

But I could hear music. A song was definitely playing. I tried to look around, focusing on the sound, but saw nothing except the darkness.

Ah, it's my radio blaring.

Indeed, my alarm was going off. My eyes bounced open as I reached to pound the snooze. Right before my fingers hit the button though, something registered; the lyrics had *pushed* loudly inside.

"Ohhhhh, you've got the best of my love. Ohhhhh, givin' you the best of my love, love." The song was, *Best of My Love,* by *The Emotions.*

With a big smile upon my face, I tapped the snooze button and then looked up at the ceiling. I acknowledged Chip.

"I do know how much you love me," I said. "And I know you'll never leave me. I know that, my darlin'. I know you can hear me. I love you so much, Chip! Thank you for being here with me."

I rolled over to my side and closed my eyes again. Off I went into slumber, beaming from the inside out.

Why Tanzania...

Originally, I had no idea where Tanzania was. I've never been a history buff nor will I ever be, but I did look it up. Tanzania is located in Africa. While researching, I learned it's also *the* location where Tanzanite diamonds are mined. With that info alone, it was all that was needed to put two and two together.

In December 2007, on Christmas Day, my future husband, Mr. Chip Oney, gave me the most beautiful engagement ring. The ring was made of... ready?... Tanzanite.

I also researched *water cow*. They do exist. The name  *water cow* is a secondary name for a pygmy hippo. And guess where the wild pygmy hippo lives? Yes, it too lives in Africa—West Africa.

Sadly, the water cows are endangered. There are less than three thousand Pygmy Hippos left in the wild. This is a picture of a baby that looks just like the little *water cow* who excitedly crammed his nose into my hand. Just look at that smile. I'm in love.

Chapter Seven

Secrets Revealed

A shock of thunderous gossip turned my world upside down. It wasn't bad enough to accept that my life was miserable and constantly dampened by tears, but now I'd been thrown into a red-hot wall of fire of crazy gossip that only seemed to be deepened by others stupidity.

I felt sick to my stomach and didn't know where to turn, what to do, or what to think.

What I really wanted was to stay high up on my mountain of hope and glory, but that wasn't meant to be. This part of my experience is shared for only one reason. Out of tragedy, no matter the kind, surprises *can* be revealed. It is not my intent to harm or hurt the feelings of anyone. Chip's truth further into this chapter, is the message that needs conveyed.

In those early days, my only avenue of connectivity to honesty, guidance, and truth was through a complete stranger. Sharing the things I encountered with certain family members or friends wasn't wise anymore. I can't count the times I was either told I wasn't moving on with my life, or I needed to let Chip go.

I ignored them all.

Secretly keeping Chip alive via my continued search for spiritual enlightenment was what I chose to do. I found and attended a Spiritual Church group every Friday night and when it was necessary, I asked for guidance from my new psychic/medium friend, Megan.

It was evident to me that Chip wanted me to focus on him, I got that, but some of the curve balls thrown my way were more than I could handle. The following e-mail conversation is based on one of those curve balls I never saw coming.

"Do you remember that song Chip sent me last week—*It's a sad, sad situation*? You told me it wasn't for me, but possibly for Chip's family. Well today, I've officially been dumped into a very sad situation. I can't breathe."

"Last night, a member of Chip's family told me they believed I showed favoritism toward him (concerning workloads). They told me Chip was dead because of me, that it's all my fault."

Chip and I worked at the same company. He was an Independent Contractor, and so was his murderer.

"This favoritism reason is so far from the truth. I'm not allowed to give deliveries to Chip or anyone else until I work my company drivers first. Whatever is left over is then given to outside carriers."

"Chip was one of *hundreds* of contractors. He hauled anything I gave him never caring what it was, and he did it without question. But now, his family believes he's no longer here because of actions that never took place."

"My heart feels like it weighs a ton today, Megan. And why would I expect anything less? Chip and I were just that— Chip and Lyn. We didn't spend much time around either of our families, so how would they really know the relationship we shared? How would they know anything about our business? They weren't there."

"They didn't know we bought a new car together, they weren't a part of our little family with our kids. They didn't ride around for hours on end with us looking for our new home. They didn't know our dreams, our goals, our plans; they didn't know anything about *us*."

"Maybe I should just wake up and figure out what I need to do with the rest of my life. Chip's not here! And I have, without question, spent these past months wrapped up in him and everything he's done from the other side. Can I really continue to do this? Can I shut a blind eye to everyone around me and continue this spiritual journey that surrounds me now? I guess that's a question only I can answer, right?"

"I wish he were still here, Megan. This is such a sad, sad situation."

I clicked the send button and walked outside to cry. I truly couldn't believe the nature of the lies and gossip I knew would leave a bad taste in many minds. Sick with a horrible headache and an extremely torn and broken heart, I knew I needed some time to think. I needed to figure things out.

Do I continue a relationship with his family? Do I keep talking to them? Do I allow them to face me and act like they care, knowing they're fake and don't care at all?

I stared up into the blue sky searching for answers as the wet, cool tears slid down my face. "Tell me what to do, my love. These are your people, not mine. Is it time to say good-bye?"

I heard nothing back and even if Chip did say something, I doubt I would have heard anything. I was too sad.

The pain of those attacking words, *it's all your fault*, trampled across my heart. Their viciousness tugged hard inside.

I wanted so badly to get angry, to strike out at the world, to lash out at his family, to my family, to my friends, to everything and everyone, but I felt too weak to do anything except cry. Today, however, time wasn't on my side.

I had to position the imaginary wall back in place. It wasn't perfected yet, but for nine hours out of the day, the wall permitted me to portray a false image of the real me. No one was allowed to see how devastated I was... the mourning widow who was living a complete and utter lie.

I wiped the tears from my face and neck, took a deep breath, and begun a forward march back to work.

Megan had responded, "The sad situation is meant for them (Chip's family). When I look to see, this is what I hear. In terms of the why Chip was killed, it had more to do with Chip and this guy. When Chip was telling me about the why, it had nothing to do with you. More that this guy had a pretty bizarre past and looks at the world through a very different lens."

"Chip had offended him somehow, by some off-handed remark. Then the guy started watching for further offenses. *Whatever you look for, you find.* Then talking about it with his friends made it bigger, and soon, they pushed him over by comments like—*are you going to let him get away with that?,* when actually there was no big thing."

"Chip does pull it toward himself, taking responsibility. All of the secrets are revealed when we pass and he got it. By some comment at some point, I was going to say when it was hot, but it's always hot there—summer or fall, Chip started it. I hope that makes sense."

"Rather than delve into the mystery of death and the unseen, the possibility there, his family would like to explain it away. It's not that simple. There must be someone at fault and if nothing will stick with the investigation, then you're the next target."

"As far as the talk, it will subside in a few days. Keep breathing and look within, that's where the truth is. This is another step in your healing and trusting yourself."

For a split second, all of the nonsense vanished. Flabbergasted, I couldn't believe what Megan had said. She had caused me to spring into a new direction of thought.

After that sinking-into-doom call last night, I had asked Chip *why.* I asked him why it began and how it all started. Could it be? The *why* she shared—is it possible? Did he just tell her... *why*?

My heart leaped in anticipation of finding out. I was oh, so cautious, yet I trusted this was going somewhere. I believed he had answered me, but I needed to be sure. No more e-mails, I picked up the phone.

I asked Megan, "Did you just get the why from Chip this morning? The part about how he's taking responsibility and that it's about this comment he made?"

"He showed me something similar before," she said. "It wasn't as clear as it was today. Before, it seemed like an exchange of some sort. The first thought I had was drug related, but that didn't resonate. Sometimes it's so hard to discern what they're saying."

"It's been longer," she continued, "and he's getting more strength and confidence. Some time when it was hot. It wasn't even a conversation, more like a comment from this big guy with serious issues. Chip mumbled something and then it was off and running. Does that make sense?"

"Yes, it makes perfect sense," I told her.

"Thinking back," she said, "he probably wouldn't have told you, but can you remember anything? It was just a big misunderstanding, but it makes more sense now how Chip kept coming to me gruff. That's how and why this all happened, keeping his mouth shut, it would have been different. But keep in mind, this is where you and his family are different. He would have left another way, not that he would still be here."

"I know," I agreed. "It's not easy to accept that it was his time to go, especially since I want him to be here, still. And you're right, Chip had no problem speaking his mind, good or bad. But that's what was so beautiful about him. You never had to worry where you stood."

"I heard how he talked to others at times," I told her. "After his outbursts, and once he calmed down, we'd discuss his actions and he'd see the error of his ways, so to speak. I do believe he was beginning to see that his sarcastic bursts weren't getting him anywhere. I always told him he couldn't talk to people the way he did. I know he did it out of frustration, but darn, he shocked me at times."

"And no," I informed her, "I don't recall Chip mentioning anything taking place between him and Vito last summer, but that was such a long time ago. I'll have to sit with it for a while and try to remember anything strange. The reason I asked you earlier about the *why*—I had a really bad episode last night. I begged Chip to tell me why this all happened."

"I was hoping it would come in a dream-visit, but I think I got the answer from you, today. Less than twenty-four hours from the time I asked him to tell me *why*, I have an answer from you. Do you remember telling me a couple of weeks ago to ask a question that I had no clue to the answer? Is this a good example of that?"

"I love this," Megan squealed, "That is so neat. I was trying to figure out a reason why it was clearer today than any other time. There's your answer."

Yes, I received my answer. Chip had indeed responded to

my question. It wasn't through a conversation with him, but it was still incredible and in some respect, seemed impossible. Yet, I was living proof it was happening.

Anytime I asked a question, I received an answer shortly thereafter. Sometimes the answers arrived like this, through Megan, sometimes through dreams, and/or sometimes through songs. It was quite amazing.

It never mattered how the answers came because when I grasped them, a magical feeling of euphoria swept through me. I still questioned many things, but I was by far much better at accepting them for what they were—*Gifts from the Afterlife.*

When that cruel phone call ended the night before, I was speechless, hurt, ashamed of his family, and feeling horribly sad for Chip at the same time.

The next day, I received this beautiful but silent message; *I'm still here.* Chip most certainly had my undivided attention now. And those horrible accusations? They no longer clouded my judgment. Instead, they disappeared with the magic of the day.

I had to ask myself, "Do I want to focus my energy on other people's stubbornness?" My answer came quite easily— *no, I do not.*

Someday, whether it's here or whether it's over there, everyone learns the truth…

Chapter Eight

I Told Him

The daily grind at work was done. It was time to release the act of pretending all was well and get back into my world of Chip. I had hoped by now it'd be easier to deal with the stress of him being gone, of him disappearing so quickly, but with the different communications in dreams and the special things he did while I was awake, I couldn't stop thinking about him.

I still missed him like crazy and *wanted* him in my life. No matter what his signs and messages were, I looked forward to each and every one.

Our bizarre connection remained a secret for the most part, though. The fear of condemnation was more problematic than I had anticipated. The last thing I needed was to be institutionalized because my dead fiancé was talking to me. So I lived two separate lives. One was in this physical world and the other was with the afterlife.

When both collided, they covered me up in a mysterious

fog of uncertainty that settled in for a spell. It was comparable to being dizzy, but only for minutes at a time. Rarely did it hamper my ability to cope with the two worlds, yet if I had my choice of which I preferred, there'd be no contest... the *other world* would win every time.

Missing Chip was never-ending. Being allowed to see him or hear him or feel him was indescribable. Letting go of *us* wasn't something I was willing to do either. Whatever needed done to continue our new relationship and to move forward with our communications, I would travel that distance.

However, some of the types of signals he gave me stunned me, and took me off guard. They shook me up and spat me out, keeping me in a state of blissful ignorance for hours at a time. Like this one, only hours after my *why* question with Megan had been answered.

After pulling into the driveway, turning the car off, jumping out, and running to the front door, I raced to the computer room. I didn't take the kids out to potty or even veer off to get a drink. This occurrence, this happening, had me dazed. My fingers landed on the keyboard to document every second.

I started writing...

Preparing to leave work, Vito's name (the shooter) popped into my head. Like all the other times, I forced him out of my mind. I refused to think about that evil man because he still creeped me out. The last thing I needed to do was dive into dreams of vengeance.

After leaving work and peacefully driving, I revisited the communications Megan had with Chip earlier in the morning. My goal was to remember *anything* Chip may have said the previous summer, like she had suggested.

With no distractions now, no phones ringing, and no one

to interrupt me, I roamed through my thoughts. But out of nowhere, they came to an unexplainable halt. When *it* happened, I had only made it around the corner from work.

So clear and loud, I heard a voice. I could have sworn the voice was sitting beside me and leaned over to say something.

"No," the male voice said. "I told him he was an idiot."

I was never so happy to be sitting at a red light. The experience of hearing *a voice* threw me into a complete state of shock. I didn't know what to do or what to say so I sat frozen like a statue, staring into the red amber. I knew it was Chip, but I didn't know how to respond. Turning my head to look at the passenger seat was a thought, but I was frightened at what I might see; I didn't dare.

I did manage to say out loud, "Wow, darlin'."

And then I swear, I heard his voice again.

He said, "I know, sweetie."

Driving all of thirty miles per hour, I sat in absolute silence. I didn't know what to say or do. Another mile down the road and at the next red light, he spoke again.

"I'm sorry," he said.

The tears suddenly formed and then I let it all out.

"Oh, my God," I yelled. "You don't have to say you're sorry, sweetie pie. You have nothing to be sorry for. You didn't do anything wrong!"

The remainder of the ride home was quiet, yet filled with thunderous thoughts.

After documenting the experience, I noticed my fingers were shaking and my body was still trembling. Newfound energy surged through me and remarkably, I felt really good. There was an incredible amount of joy inside that had somehow rolled itself up into one big bundle of unexplained emotions.

After taking a deep breath, I sat back in the chair. Reliving the phenomenal experience soared me into the clouds of wonder, and then the plummet back to reality took the delight completely away. I was such a doubter. That's who I was, the big skeptic.

Surely, I wanted to believe I was communicating with my sweetheart, but seriously, who does that? Other than mediums and intuitives, who communicates with dead people? Not me.

This was different though. I felt it in my bones. It was more real, more alive, than anything I'd experienced before. Even if it was a brief moment in time, I *knew* I felt Chip there. His presence, his energy, his personality, his love, it was all there... sitting beside me in that car.

"I have to change my perspective and trust him," I told myself. "I know this secret—the Afterlife is very real."

Time suddenly became nothing. It was easy to sit inside the new wisdom and lose myself inside of it. Today, validations were not needed and reality stood close by. It was time to get back to it; our kids.

While they pranced around outside, I breathed in the fresh air on top of the cool breeze. Staring up into the beautiful blue sky, I became empty of all words and all questions.

Time became... a perfect texture of nothingness.

Chapter Nine

He's My Brother

With the economy in shambles and so many people unemployed, it was no surprise I found myself standing in Wal-Mart feeling a ton of empathy for a woman sitting far off in the distance. She looked distraught and alone.

In an instant though, I had an unexpected pull, a knowing of sorts, that I needed to go toward the deli. Before anything else was allowed to roam through my head, my feet kicked in and I was on the move, leaving the pharmacy. It never dawned on me to question why I needed to go there.

On the way, I noticed a kiosk filled with candy bars sitting in the middle of the isle. A few steps later, I noticed a second one identical to the first. When I walked up to the third kiosk, also filled with candy, I couldn't help but laugh and reached in to pick up a Snickers.

"Chip loves candy bars," I whispered. "It's a good thing he's not here cause he'd be loading up on 'em."

Out of nowhere, like magic, Chip appeared. Just like that, he was standing beside me.

"Grab one of each, darlin," he excitedly said.

So I did, happily. I nabbed three and never asked where Chip had come from, and it didn't seem to matter. His death never entered the equation. For that matter, it never happened.

Nonchalantly, we walked to the deli. I followed behind Chip, checking out his broad shoulders and admiring his stature. He stood tall, his head rotating as he continued to walk unusually slow and browsing the food on the counters. His hair was shiny, freshly trimmed, and looked silky smooth.

Around the counters and shelves we explored. It wasn't long before I started to wonder why we hadn't picked up a single thing. Nothing. My curiosity beckoned loudly, "Why are we walking in circles?" Before the words could escape my lips however, I saw that lady again. She was still sitting near the registers with her head lowered, looking so sad.

I stopped dead in my tracks and scratched my head. "What are we doing here?"

For the life of me, I couldn't understand why we were there, in Wal-Mart, trotting around, yet not buying anything. Nothing was making sense. Suddenly, Chip took my hand and pulled me, almost jerking my arm out of socket, into a different direction.

He was rushing us down a vacant corridor. Glancing up, I was engrossed with the beauty of the entryway. It was decorated with extra-large white castlewall stones, was old-timey looking, yet it was very elegantly designed. The hallway was enormous and we were the only ones there.

Hanging high up in the air was a sign that read, Bar/Restaurant, and I caught another word scrawled across the top—Seafood.

"What a fantastic surprise," I said, while Chip tugged my hand, dragging me. "This is a brilliant idea."

We undeniably loved our seafood. I clutched Chip's arm,

laid my head on top of his shoulder and sighed a beautiful sigh of delight. I didn't want to seem too anxious, too excited, or even too hungry, but I was starving and couldn't wait to eat.

We had reached two oversized, beautifully stained-glass entrance doors when Chip escorted me through. My head was still in the clouds, but right before we entered the restaurant, I glanced at that sign once more.

"Why hasn't Wal-Mart thought of this idea before now? It's a marvelous addition."

Chip added our name, Oney, to the waiting list. It was going to be a few minutes before we could be seated so I led him to the waiting area and scoped out a couple of secluded seats. All that was there was a very long bench taking up the entire length of the wall. It was extremely dark in color, brown maybe. I walked us to the end of the waiting room, in the corner, and then turned to take a seat.

When I lifted my eyes to meet Chip's, it was no longer Chip I saw. Instead, the face in front of me was the face of an old boyfriend, Jerry. Jerry wasn't someone I seriously dated, so I was quite stunned to see him. I wanted to gasp for air, but instead, I held my breath. I didn't want to hurt his feelings, yet I wondered if he could sense how unhappy I was to see him. To my complete surprise, he plopped down and sat on the bench beside me.

Life was challenging as of late, I had to admit that. At times, I found it almost impossible to ascertain which reality I was in; awake or asleep. Right now, I couldn't be sure.

"Maybe I turned Jerry into Chip somehow. Maybe because I want Chip here so badly, and I've wished for it so hard, my crazy eyes morphed Jerry into Chip."

"But I broke it off with Jerry," I started to remember. "Right?"

All of a sudden, Jerry started to play. His upper body moved toward my lap, but he kept his brown eyes linked to mine. His hand lifted the top of my dress as he took a quick peek.

"Let me see under your dress," he whispered.

"Wait a minute," I thought. "Chip's the one who says that, not Jerry. Is this really Jerry here?"

He started tickling me and I couldn't help it, I laughed. We joked and played, and I giggled out loud. Joy and fun had taken over and those doubtful thoughts all but disappeared.

"All is okay, I'm with Jerry, not Chip," I finally had it figured it out. "Chip never died. I must have made it all up."

As soon as I became comfortable with my conclusion, Jerry pulled away and leaped in front of my face. But it wasn't Jerry I saw. This time, it was Chip.

Startled, I jumped back. All I could do was stare. I gaped at his large smile as it drew me in, captivating me. Before I knew it, everything was gone. My thoughts were wiped from my mind and momentarily erased.

It was Chip and me, in love. His love was so strong I could touch it. It was so powerful, it overwhelmed me and the tears began their descent. Every ounce of him—his essence, his true self, his heart, his voice—I felt him. He blended like the sound of a small drum beating inside of my heart. My breath had been taken away.

All that mattered was now. Right here. This very moment.

This instant where I wrapped my arms around him and held him tight against me. Where my hand embraced his head while his soft lips gently caressed and kissed my neck. Where I felt his warm body against mine and where I experienced nothing but the love he had for me.

My heart spillethed over. My tears bled for my true love.

Nothing mattered in our little corner of the world. Not even the commotion in the distance. The physicalness of being inside his arms and knowing it was him, my sweet love, blanketed us in complete and utter Bliss.

"Why did I turn him into Jerry?" I asked myself. "Have I lost my mind?"

Chip's wide shoulders blocked the view of everything surrounding me. He had me pinned in with my back pressed tightly against the wall. I felt a little anxious... I sensed someone staring at us and I needed to take a look.

But then Chip tickled me again and started kissing me all over the face, obstructing everything. His distraction worked; my focus was back on him. I was hoping we weren't making a big scene, but I had a sense that we were. I also had a nagging feeling that someone was watching our every move. An uncontrollable urge was begging me to take a peek.

Chip's face was now buried in my neck, keeping me from seeing anything—he was showering me with wet kisses. With my hands gripping his shoulders, I tried to scoot him to the left. It took some doing, but he finally got the non-subtle hint and removed himself from my neck and sat down beside me.

All of a sudden, Jerry, not Chip, sprung back on top of me. But not before I caught that glimpse. There was someone standing in the entrance watching us and now, my gut was telling me he was walking toward us.

Instinctively, I knew the stranger didn't check in or put his name on the waiting list. Somehow, I knew he opened the door and immediately entered the sitting area. He was there, standing feet away, waiting for me to acknowledge him; waiting for me to see him.

The only problem with that, however, was Jerry. He was covering me up like Chip did and being very playful. My irritation with him was growing by leaps and bounds. I tried to push him off to no avail. I screamed at him to get off, insisting he move.

After a few more minutes of struggle, I was finally allowed to lean over and peer through his arm. I saw the stranger's feet clearly—and then he took one step to his left to be more visible. Unfortunately, all I could see was his lower body.

His pants were chocolate brown and they had white speckled spots, too. From the hem near his shoes all the way up to his waist, his pants were covered in tiny white dots.

Suddenly, Jerry scooted out of the way and I could see the stranger fully. But what was registering in my eyes wasn't clicking very well. This wasn't something that sat okay with me. It wasn't good.

The stranger stood tall with his shoulders back. His arms were draped by his side and in his left hand, he was holding a damn gun. "He's so young," I told myself. "And handsome, too. Why does he feel he needs to do this?"

The next thing I knew, Jerry extended his arm across my waist, pinning me in again. He wouldn't allow me to get up to help the stranger. I stretched my arm out as far as I could, reaching for him. I needed to help him, to stop him, from taking his life.

I yelled at him, "Noooooooooooooooooooooooo! No, no, no!"

The mysterious man gazed into my eyes when the strangest thing happened—I became silent. Unexpectedly, his hypnotic eyes of blue quieted me. His dirty blond hair was thick and sloppy and his eyes were freakishly glued to mine.

The stranger's hand wiggled and then slowly, he lifted the gun and placed the barrel next to his head. I could hear him talking to me inside my mind.

"Follow my other hand," he said. I did as he asked.

Our eyes remained synched with each other, but at the same time, I watched his hand rise. Midway up in front of his chest, it stopped. After forming a fist, he lifted one finger. Next, his middle finger rose and quickly thereafter, he lifted his ring finger, too. While he raised each finger, he also counted, out loud, "One. Two. Three."

Swiftly, he pulled the trigger. The gun went off twice. I heard two distinctive gun shots. As his body fell to the floor, his blood spilled everywhere. Bounding away from the bench, I ran as fast as I could toward the door, passing his lifeless body. As rapidly as I could, I pulled out my cell and tried to dial 911. But the call wouldn't go through.

"God no," I discouragingly screamed. "Not this again!"

I was a frantic mess and couldn't believe it was all happening yet again. I ran through the restaurant to the front door, but suddenly felt Jerry's presence. When I turned to look, I saw him racing toward me, holding the gun.

"Why do you have the gun, Jerry?" I yelled. "The police are going to think you shot him."

He was freaking out, too. He turned and ran back to the stranger's body and released the gun from his grasp. Helping Jerry wasn't my priority at the moment; I needed to assist the stranger. Spinning away, I headed back to the front door needing to get reception for my phone.

It was useless. My cell wasn't working and the scene was all too familiar. I had done this exact same thing with Chip. The identical sinking feelings of being alone and frightened were slapping me in the face all over again.

"I can't do this," I cried out. "I just can't do this."

Behind my eyes, the tears were forcefully welling up, ready to stream across my cheeks. I stared at my cell vacantly, unable to move and ready to give up.

Out of nowhere, I heard a woman's voice coming near. She was reaching out for me. Gently, she took my hand and pressed it to her chest. Tenderly, she placed her phone in my palm and folded my fingers around it.

"Here," her angelic voice said. "Use this one to call 911. You'll be able to get through. I promise."

"Thank you," I replied, and turned the phone over. Speedily, I punched the keypad ... 9 1 1.

In the blink of an eye... everything turned to black. The overwhelming loud sound of silence thumped hard inside my head. Remnants of sweat drenched my body; its cool chill gliding across my skin.

In a matter of seconds, I knew it. I had awakened from a dream. Another one of those visions where it didn't feel like a dream at all. This one, it was different and very powerful.

Remaining completely still in bed, I spent every second going over the details and recording everything in my mind so I could document it later. I had only recently noticed the physicalness in my dreams and when I felt something tangible, it was a sign for me to pay full attention.

The candy bars were solid. I felt the weight of them in my hand. Chip kissing me all over the face and neck; I felt the warmth of his breath and the softness of his lips, too. There was no difference in his touch, none. Yes, I felt him physically again. No question about it. The stranger, however? No clue who he was.

"This isn't right," I said out loud. "That world is more real. This one here, feels more like the dream."

I chose not to share this *dream-visit* right away. If I was to grow and discern the dreams for myself, sharing them wasn't going to help me. So, I wrote everything down, reading it over and over again. Diving into the details, I searched to find my personal connection to the stranger. I didn't know how I knew him, but I knew there was a connection somewhere and I truly desired to figure it out.

Over the next couple of days however, I discovered nothing new. Even though I was disappointed in my discernment, I also knew I needed to give myself a break. This was a new life and not something I had been programmed to do for years. It was going to take some time to get it all sorted out, if that was even possible.

A few days later, I decided to get in touch with Megan. It was time to ask for help.

"Everything was so darn vivid," I told her. "I saw Chip and then I didn't. I was with him, and then I wasn't. What was really crazy was how someone from my past kept mixing all in. The man who shot himself though, I remember looking at his face, staring into his eyes."

"He was so determined to shoot himself in front of me. Right there, so I could watch him and everything else he did too. Why on earth would Chip share something like that? What am I supposed to learn from this?"

Megan consoled me, "I feel like it's more symbolic of how you're feeling about Chip leaving; there, not there, etc. Like the bathrooms, your internal self, your plumbing so to speak, but not literally. Not your own death, but changes, life changes. And transformations, I'm also getting the picture of butterflies. This can be a big positive change."

Megan stopped for a moment before she continued. "The man who shot himself sounded familiar. I'm trying to place him, but related somehow to Chip. He's tall, blond, has Germanic features, yes?"

The energy exploding from her words sent chills all across

my body. Yes! The stranger did have German traits. My heart raced crazily because I was thrilled she had picked up on him.

I sat for a second longer, thinking, knowing I, too, had looked at the many comparisons between Chip's murder and the dream-visit. It all tied together, especially the one-two-three. For heaven's sake, Chip died on 1/23. And the cell phone issue... not being able to get through... hello? I understood what she said *but that man,* there was something about him. I couldn't let him go and I didn't know why.

A part of me was in complete awe of the dreams lately, but another part of me, not so much. They made me feel like a fish out of water. The dreams were so real, so alive; they seriously felt like an extension of me somehow. They made me wonder if there was an existence somewhere else and I was just as real there, just as alive, as I am here. Yet, on this side of the scope, the dreams were very confusing.

"Yes, he does have German traits," I responded. "I know this probably doesn't matter, but I memorized his pants. They were chocolate brown with little white speckles. They reminded me of the 70s era, but in the here and now. And he did the counting, the raising of the gun, and the pulling of the trigger with such a purpose. Like he was saying, *this is what I'm going to do and nothing or no one is going to stop me.*"

Right then, the world came to a stop, instantly. Her words, *Germanic features,* started a war inside my head, tapping all over my thoughts. And then there it was. The magic light bulb moment.

"Oh … my … God!" I screamed. "I know who he is! I know who he is! Megan, he's my brother, Billy. I think the year was 1985—he committed suicide, shooting himself in the head. And, we are part German."

She sat and listened to my interpretation.

"I told Chip all about Billy. After Charlie, my Chihuahua, died, we had several conversations about him. Why wouldn't Chip be a part of Billy now, or vice versa?"

"Oh, oh, wait," my excitement was over the top. "Billy died on Valentine's Day. I'm almost sure of it. That would explain the chocolate brown pants with the white speckles—a symbol for chocolate candy."

"Oh, wow," Megan cried out. "He was coming through to me on my medium call on Monday, I just couldn't place him. The counting is sometimes how I can tell if it's a sudden death or an illness, in how they count. A slow one, two, three, is usually an illness. Quick, especially a fast 123, was how he showed me. I asked him to have his family find me. Wow."

Valentine's Day, Billy's transition day. Chip and Billy were very creative, little boogers. Even though it freaked me out and scared me to death, I had to admit, I could see every detail of the choreography they created.

When Megan told Billy to have his family find her, I imagine Billy and Chip were charged up, knowing exactly what was about to happen. It was just a matter of time before their plot pleasingly unfolded.

Bad, bad, boys... yes, they were.

As a side note, I recently learned that Valentine's Day is *not* the day my brother passed. Over the years, I somehow connected him to that day and since that's what I believed, he and Chip used that information for recognition purposes. Billy actually passed away on 2/13, not 2/14.

Even after I learned of this new date, I never put it together. Not until I saw a commercial one afternoon where the numbers 213 were shown in the background. I leaped from my chair and shouted, "Holy crap. Billy has the same numbers as Chip... 123."

That's when the larger picture hit me. None of this happened by chance. There's a reason for the *123* connection. It's now my job to figure it out.

Chapter Ten

Follow Your Dreams

One evening, I decided to go to bed rather early. A cold was trying to dig in and I figured rest might stop it. It didn't take too long to fall asleep.

In only minutes, it seemed, I heard my voice dance through the darkness of the room. Reciting medical notes, I was saying things I knew absolutely nothing about. Seconds later and once my awareness kicked in, I knew the words belonged to a doctor.

Moments earlier, his journal sat inside my hands. *Ants destroyed their nasal cavity*, he wrote. Two young boys had died and their official cause of death was from ants.

The coolness of his workplace lingered. I stood in an office that felt more like a home, a much older dwelling, with a desk that sat in front of a window overlooking the grounds. I peered out, questioning, *where am I,* and then before I knew it, I was back in bed.

"Why did I have that dream?" I whispered into the dark. "Why was I reading that doctor's notes? And what on earth was the purpose?"

Recently, I read that dreams were meant to teach us what our soul desires along life's path. They help us by giving us hints and clues about what we're to learn or even to teach. However, this dream didn't feel like one of those. Somehow I had brought it back here in my physical world. Like that of the extension I mentioned earlier, both worlds colliding.

Asking again, out loud, I knew I needed more help.

"What am I supposed to learn from this?" But the only thing I heard back was a quote that raced across my thoughts. It was from the Bible; *ask and ye shall receive.*

There was nothing else; no physical form or voice and I hurriedly convinced myself I needed to go back to sleep. The way I figured it, if I was there in that other world, maybe I could discover more answers. Closing my eyes tightly, I waited for my mind to fade away.

Infiniti was written on a dark blue dashboard.

"Ah, this car, my surroundings," I recognized the gold words. "I know where I am."

I didn't have to turn my head, I felt Chip sitting beside me.

"Oh, I get it now," I discerned. "We're in our new Infiniti we bought in January." My eyes were glued to the dashboard. "Okay, everything feels normal, just as it should be. Nothing has changed, right?"

The weight of Chip's hand was warm and resting on top of my leg. Slowly, I turned my head and prayed I wasn't dreaming. He was sitting there, so handsomely.

His eyes met mine and suddenly, I felt like I was home. He looked happy as I watched his pouty lips crawl into a large gentle smile.

His left hand was resting on top of the steering wheel. Everything was exactly the same. The only thing off was me; I missed him badly. The love that I felt from him was nothing short of elation. It was so strong I had to turn and stare out the window before the tears exploded from my eyes.

"Whew," I thought. "He's not dead. He's right here. Damn, that was a bad nightmare. Seeing him get murdered like that! And believing it was real? I dare not share this one with him. He'll freak out on me again and tell me I need to go and see a doctor about my dreams."

"No," I told myself. "I have to keep this one a secret. Besides, it really doesn't matter now anyway. It was all just a really, really, frightening dream. Good lord, why would I think up such a horrific death for him?"

Unexpectedly, the car hit a speed-bump, and then another. When I looked up, I recognized everything. I saw the mailboxes, the houses, the dog... awww look, it's Mrs. Benton's pooch. I recognized the flowers, the big willow tree, I knew exactly where I was; we were on our way to Chip's house.

It was amazing how good I felt. It was intense, but exceptional. Bigger than anything I'd ever known before, this was grand love and on a much higher scale. Chip had taken over my heart and I was more in love with him than ever.

"I feel so freaking alive!" I said, to myself.

"How can I miss him so badly if his death was only a nightmare?" I stared down at his hand again and then thought, "I think I have some serious issues I need to deal with."

Chip's house was right around the corner. We would be there shortly, but I wasn't sure why we were headed there. Maybe we were picking up his mom.

After he put the car in park, I opened the door and stepped out. Chip was already several feet ahead of me. I caught myself staring at his clothes because his attire wasn't normal. His dress code was immaculate and not something he usually wore.

"I've never seen that suit before," I whispered.

His suit was neatly pressed, not a wrinkle in sight. It was a bright black, almost blindingly bright. And his blond hair was popping and beaming in the sunlight.

"Damn, he looks good," I said.

Chip had moved so quickly as I watched him climb one step up to the front door, or I had moved too slowly; I was still at the car. I had fallen far behind, yet I couldn't take my eyes off of him.

His right hand held the metal railing as he turned and stared into my eyes. The sight of him rendered me helpless. I was literally breathless, speechless, and frozen in time.

A flash of white sparkled brilliantly from his shirt underneath his jacket. He looked staggeringly handsome and I was smothered in admiration as my love for him pressed strongly against my chest. When he smiled, both corners of his full lips wrinkled with delicious delight. I smiled back.

Suddenly, the wind ruffled my dress at my knees, distracting me. The need to look down was strong and when I did, I wrestled with my dress. And then it hit me, "Why am I wearing this?"

It was the same outfit I wore to Chip's funeral service. "We don't match, I'm not wearing black. Why?" The frustration sank in. "Darn it, Lyn, you should have worn the dress he bought you, why didn't you?"

I lifted my head to find Chip. He had climbed two more steps and only had one more to go before he reached the front door. For some reason, I felt the urge to look at his shoes. On his final step up, his shiny slacks rose up off of his ankle sending a wave of shock that pierced me. I gasped for air, surprised at what my eyes beheld.

Chip was wearing black leather shoes. But they weren't

brand new like his suit. No, these were very old. As I studied them, searching every discolored and tattered line in its entirety, I couldn't figure out why he was wearing such old wrinkled up shoes.

When it came to his attire, Chip was worse than a woman. He had dozens of new shoes he hadn't worn yet. But these... they didn't make sense.

"Why is he wearing those shoes with that smashing suit?"

Upon reaching the staircase, I rapidly realized I wasn't allowed to accompany him inside. I didn't question it really and simply stood and waited. Chip opened the door slowly and I watched it inch forward into the house. He took one step inside and then turned to face me.

Once again, his smile covered his face as I became mesmerized, hypnotized. His eyes were talking to me and I was completely at ease, at peace. I was wholly loved and I trusted he'd return shortly.

He closed the door slowly, smiling and hanging his face out the crack until he had to move. I watched the door close and stood alone, waiting.

With his mother in tow, we each climbed into her car. Where we were heading I didn't know, but we were all going together. Chip got into the driver's seat while I hopped into the passenger side. His mom sat in the back, in the middle, and was carrying on with Chip. She wasn't a happy camper that we were riding in her car and wanted to know why, when he and I had two newer vehicles. I couldn't say I didn't wonder it, too; it was a rather good question.

They went on and on about it, like a never-ending story. I sat in silence, letting the two of them duke it out while laughing at their antics. They were so funny together, neither one willing to give up their belief and each saying anything to make their point heard. I laughed at them for a while, but then I blocked them out.

A building ahead had become my focal point, a considerably large funeral home.

"Why are we going there?" I wondered.

Chip rested his hand on top of my lap while my attention remained ahead. The building was getting closer and closer while I yearned to see more. He made a left-hand turn into the large entrance and ever so gradually, we inched forward. The silence inside the car was extremely loud, but I didn't care. Suddenly, Chip's voice roamed through my ears.

"You know those two little boys who died from the ants in their nasal cavity?" he asked, while gently slapping my lap.

"Yes?" I responded.

"We're here to attend their funeral," he said.

My body jerked and my eyes flew open. As soon as his words ripped through my ear, I was wide awake, and very disappointed. I wanted badly to attend the funeral.

Instead of saying, *Lyn, this was a dream, silly girl. Get real,* I proposed a different question altogether and asked it out loud.

"What's their connection to you, Chip? Why are they so important to you? And why were we going to their funeral?"

He had me, completely. I believed with all my heart I was seeing something real. Something no one else could see.

But this time there were no quotes, no voices, no anything to my waywardly questions. It was only midnight and I knew the likelihood of Chip appearing was pretty slim to none. I was still very tired and knew I needed to get back to sleep.

So I closed my eyes again…

Chip had disappeared. We were in the car heading to Waldo, a small town outside of Jacksonville, when he pulled into a grocery store. As I opened the door and stepped out, I noticed that he had vanished. This wasn't the first time he'd disappeared on me, so I wasn't the least bit surprised. Long ago, I learned if I didn't stay close by, I usually had to wait for him to find me. Chip loved to shop... and would vanish in an instant.

I decided to walk over to the entrance of the store. Upon stepping up onto the sidewalk, out of nowhere Chip appeared. But he wasn't alone. He had a lady on his arm.

"Lynnie, look who I found," he shouted loudly. "It's Kim!" His thunderous laughter could be heard a mile away and I recognized her instantly.

"I know it's Kim, silly man," I said as we raced toward each other.

It was a glorious reunion as we gave each other a big southern hug. I was so excited Kim was there. I didn't exactly know why she was, but nonetheless, I was thrilled just the same.

We each turned, locked arms, in sync, and headed to the entrance of the store. We were laughing, skipping, and having a grand time. The doors slid open and as we began to enter, a woman appeared. I knew her, too. Happily, we all hugged each other. I was thrilled. But then she said something that shook me up.

"It's so good to see both of you together again," she yelled. "You guys did the right thing by waiting until now. You can be together now and be open about your relationship."

My heart felt warm with joy and at the same time, I saw the pleasure of her words on Chip's face. His smile radiated happiness, but I couldn't help myself, I questioned her remark. "Why would she say that?" I aske myself. "We haven't split up. We've been together all this time. We've always been *together."*

Dazed and confused, I felt Chip tugging at my arm, wanting us to walk outside. As we exited the doors, interestingly enough, we ran into another lady, and then another. The reception was the same from each woman and their words were almost identical as before.

"We're so glad you're together and free to express yourselves now," one of them said. "We're so happy for you two!" the other shouted.

I stood in conversation with each of them and stared at their beautiful faces, but their words dug in and haunted me.

"Seriously, why did they say that?" I whispered.

In a flash, I was back in my bed and rolling over.

"I'm awake again? What's up with that?"

The women's voices hung in the air, their words skipping through my thoughts; *we're so happy for you two... you're free to express your feelings now.* I knew all of them, but I couldn't quite figure out how, exactly.

"They're alive, here with me in this physical world, right?" I questioned, out loud. And then I heard Chip's voice suddenly dart across the room.

"They're the women at the beauty salon, silly," he said.

Aha. That's it. They all worked at the salon where we got our hair done together. These were the women, the only people we knew, who knew the real *us* because we kept our relationship secret from most everyone.

What a relief. I finally figured out a dream. Sure, I understood I had a little help from a voice that wasn't mine. Chip was talking to me again and this time, solved a puzzle.

At first, I thought about fearing what I heard, but quickly realized there wasn't anything to be afraid of. Besides, why should I fear love? And why did it matter so much that I could talk to my sweetheart in the afterlife? It wasn't like I was going to tell anyone anyway. This was our little secret.

While I stared at the ceiling, I decided to ask Chip a question. "Chip, why did those women say what they said? Why is it okay for us to be together now, when we can't really be together? You're dead, Chip! It's not possible."

Before I knew it, my mind slipped away again…

Surprised was an understatement when I found myself remembering this man's name without hesitation; Don Zutell. Don was a driver and a friend from a very distant past employer, and someone I knew for a fact Chip didn't know.

"What the hell? I haven't seen this man in twenty plus years, right?" I said, to myself.

There he was in front of me, still carrying his full head of white hair. His smile was contagious as ever, his posture excellent, and that New York accent still very strong; it was tough understanding him.

Don was an older man way back then and one whom held my greatest respect. He was brutally honest and had the biggest heart of any gentle man I knew. But at the moment, his voice only distracted my thoughts from figuring out where we were.

Next to a large body of water and in the middle of a construction site, we were standing on top of a dock somewhere. Don didn't seem to care though. He was very wordy about something and making it difficult to grasp anything familiar. What I wanted to do was scream at him— where am I?—but he wasn't allowing me a word in edgewise.

When I twirled my head from the water, my heart fluttered, skipping a full beat. Chip was walking toward us and beside him was a little dog, too.

"Now where did Chip pick him up?" I asked myself.

He walked up and gave me a nice kiss and then I leaned down to smother the cute pooch with some affection. The dog was such a loving little guy and thoroughly enjoyed getting his belly rubbed.

It seemed Chip knew Don quite well. The two of them were conversing as though they'd known each other all their lives, and were acting like I wasn't even there.

Several minutes passed when I decided to look up. The distance between us had grown some, but I stayed put and kept playing with the dog. I never wanted Chip to think I needed to be in his business, so I always made sure he had his space. When he was ready to include me, he'd come and get me. He always did.

As I stood from petting the pup, I watched as Chip strode toward me taking very large steps and swinging his arms proudly. He picked me up and hugged me tightly as my laughter roared. After placing me down, he surprised me when his face flew in front of my mine.

He wrapped his hands around my face and gently held me front and center. His bright blue eyes gazed deeply into my soul before his lips moved over mine, passionately kissing me, taking my breath away.

Unexpectedly, that New York accent collapsed the sweet moment when he hollered out, "I knew you two were a couple. I just knew it. It's so good to see you guys together and happy. I'm so happy for you both."

Chip released his hold and dropped his arm around my waist, keeping me firmly against him. The two of them continued to talk business while I stood right there in the middle. That was exactly what I didn't like, being inside of their conversation. Suddenly, from somewhere out in left field, Chip convinced himself that his crazy idea was sane.

"I'm calling your boss right now," he told Don. "He can't treat his employees like this. I'll tell him a thing or two."

Chip pulled out his cell phone from his jacket pocket and lifted it waist-high. He dialed the number and at the same time, recited his speech. Don interrupted him and said, "No, man. you can't say that! That'll be too hard."

Chip's eyes then moved to mine, but he didn't say anything. He didn't have to. I knew what he wanted—to agree or disagree with him. All I had inside was a huge urge to bite my tongue. If I disagreed, I'd only hurt his feelings so I pretended to ignore his advance altogether. Instead, I leaned down to pet the dog again and prayed he'd leave me out of this one.

But the quietness was loud. They weren't talking. When I looked up to find out why, both of them were staring at me. Their silence spoke volumes, Chip wanted me to respond. So I took a very deep breath before speaking.

"Sweetie, you were," I hesitated briefly, "a little too hard."

In the blink of an eye, Chip burst into laughter. His head swung back, his arms flew up and he belly laughed, loudly. He was so loud, I was stunned.

Why is he laughing? I wondered.

I didn't understand what I said that was so darn funny, and at the same time, I felt my irritation growing, too. I stood from petting the dog and when I did, Chip reached over and held my face in his hands again. His lips slammed onto mine when he gave me one of the biggest, the strongest, and the best kisses he'd ever given me.

He literally stole my breath and while staring into his eyes, I had to ask him, "What the heck was that for?"

But in a flash, like magic, he disappeared. Chip was gone.

And I was left lying in bed all alone.

"What the heck's going on?" I questioned, out loud. It wasn't every night I woke from several different dreams and all of them so darn vivid.

"Why do you laugh at me like that?" I asked.

I seriously didn't see the humor like he did.

"All of these dreams aren't normal, are they?" I was worried again, about being or going crazy.

"Hell, what's normal about any of this?"

Waiting for a response from Chip, from anyone actually, I stared at the ceiling again. One word, two words, anything really. It didn't matter. All I needed was to hear something. Sadly though, there was nothing but silence.

The night of mystery was over.

Contemplating my sanity yet again, I rolled over in frustration and asked myself, "Does everyone have dreams like these? If they do, how in the world do they deal with them?"

The next morning, I made it a priority to find out. I needed to know if I was normal. I needed to talk to Megan.

"Does he laugh at me because when he gets me in these dreams I haven't a clue they're dreams?" I asked her. "Is it because he finds humor in the delicate manner in which I still try to correct him? I can't figure him out."

"Your dreams are interesting," Megan said. "He makes a point of showing you his shoes which are worn out. The suit reminds me of that movie, *Meet Joe Black;* I feel like it's another reminder that his agreement was up. This part of his *life* was over, thus moving onto the other side."

"As for the boys, the ants in *Animal Medicine* don't come up. But it feels to me like living in the ant hill, being part of a community. The two of you never felt like you could be a part of the community together, having to hide yourselves. Lyn, I swear, when you get there, even if it's fifty years from now, it will seem like only fifteen minutes has passed."

"God, I hope so," I responded. "What do you think about him laughing at me like that? That really baffles me."

"I don't feel like he's laughing *at* you, but just that all is well. Things are as they should be. He adjusted so quickly to the way things are and is with many loved ones. I also feel like he's taken on his job, too. Something about welcoming others over, spending time with them and helping them adjust. And it's loved ones, family, and *odd*, senseless deaths; Military maybe? That would make sense given who he is."

"He reminds me of the guy on the train in *Ghost,*" she added. "The one who teaches Patrick Swayze's character to move things. *Look at what I can do, look at how I contact my baby... you can, too.*"

After hanging up, I could hear his laughter again, or so I thought I did. I loved Chip's laugh. It was always so rich and authentic. We laughed a lot and found humor in everything we did, so maybe Megan was right. He wasn't laughing *at* me, he was laughing because everything *was* okay and as it should be.

Something about her comparison to *Meet Joe Black* felt powerful for me as well. I don't know if it was the movie itself or if the old shoes seemed to fit more snugly, but it seemed like Chip was Joe Black for those few moments. Either way, I agreed. His physical agreement had been completed and his old shoes firmly confirmed that.

I never asked her if this kind of dreaming was normal. As the years passed, however, I learned that it wasn't, not really. A lot of people didn't remember their dreams and those that did, didn't truly study them. Preceding Chip's death, I couldn't recall dreaming much at all. This was, for the most part, brand new and sometimes it felt more like a jigsaw puzzle than anything else. The perfect example was this night of dreams.

1. Two young boys died because *ants* destroyed their nasal cavity. *Ants* being the symbol to the puzzle.

2. Chip took on his *new job* helping others cross over who experienced a *senseless or sudden death.*

3. The women and the friend, Don Zutell, expressed happiness in seeing us together again in the *community.*

In its simplest form, the ants symbolized us being a part of the community. The two young boys who died were who Chip helped to cross over; his new job in the Afterlife. The women and friend, Don, were a clear indication we were meant to communicate this way. Everything was out in the open now and we didn't have to hide anything.

I could see Chip being the go-to guy, the one who teaches other souls how to do certain things in order to communicate with this side. It *fits* him well since he loved to teach when he was here on this side.

"He reminds me of the guy on the train in Ghost that teaches Patrick Swayze's character to move things. Look at what I can do, look at how I contact my baby. You can, too."

Chapter Eleven

Shower Me With Love

I had always believed in fate. I knew Chip and I were together for a reason, even if I didn't know what that reason was. Having experienced déjà vu's all of my life and feeling like I was doing exactly what I was supposed to be doing, there were many times I believed Chip and I were brought together to experience an extraordinary love.

After many years of getting burned, one's views of an everlasting love can often disintegrate. Chip believed he needed to change my mind and redeem the male species. I agreed with him—men were wrapped up into one or two bad categories but for some, rightly so. With him though, it became a priority to convert me.

Since he knew tidbits of my past, he was aware that my luck in love wasn't a blessed one and that my faith in men pretty much sucked. But what surprised me the most about him was knowing that his past relationships didn't survive any more than mine, yet, he *insisted* on showing me that *his* love was capable of crashing my walls of protection.

He prided himself on proving that not all men were the

same. It was all he talked about. He wanted to guide me into a wonderful, fun, loving friendship and a very, very special relationship. I never got the chance to tell him he succeeded.

Chip never gave up on me. Even when he had plenty of reasons to. In the beginning, I fought his advances, I ignored his calls, and I stood him up more times than I care to count. It wasn't because of him that I did that. It was because of a strong and eerie feeling that told me he'd hurt me if I got too close.

As far as I was concerned, I had completed a life long journey experiencing abusive relationships. There would be no more. Period. I knew that loving myself was more important than letting someone else demean me, rule me, or change me. Back then, I didn't know it, but Chip wasn't capable of doing anything bad.

And what I feared most, him hurting me, was exactly what happened. No, he didn't intentionally hurt me and no, he didn't abuse me. But his death—his physical death—killed me, too. Right there beside him, I died.

Heartbreak via Chip, all came true.

Chip brought me back to life in those short years together. There were tons of things to remember him by, then and now. What I missed the most was our laughing at the silliest of things. And not having my best friend by my side every day was the hardest to get used to.

Not only was the grief bad, nothing in my life felt right. I didn't seem to *fit* anywhere. Not in my body, not in this life… nowhere. I often appeared as an existing zombie going through the motions. I even wondered at times if I lived in some type of *Matrix* system and my *real* life was someplace else.

I read somewhere, *this physical life is an illusion and where we really come from is much more magical and beautiful.* It didn't take but a second to snatch up that quote and make it my own.

Illusion—the word that started a change and the altering of my perspective about everything. Since the dream-visits seemed more alive than my human life, it got me to thinking.

Is it true? Is life an illusion? I experimented with the theory for a time and still do to an extent.

For example: One afternoon, I was riding the mower in my very *bumpy* yard getting knocked around when the question slipped out. "So this is an illusion?"

Another time, Scooby decided to shake his paw, but missed my hand and instead scraped my leg. I couldn't help but ask, "So that was an illusion?"

One more example was when I decided to wash my car in the rain, getting soaked. I stopped, looked up the best I could, and asked, "This is an illusion, too? How can that be?"

There was no direct answer heard, but I did listen to what I thought to be lots of laughter. I guess *they* figured I was being funny or something.

Inside of my *Matrix* theory was where I found myself asking more serious questions though.

"Why did I choose to be here? Why did I choose to suffer his murder? Why did I agree to let Chip die?" Agree—as in soul contracts.

My heart wanted to stay in the mix of our love, but when I looked around at the wicked evil in the world I couldn't help but wonder, *why is there so much hurt around us?*

This was when I changed and decided not to focus on the evil, but to concentrate on all the good life had to offer. This was when I strong-willed myself and transformed what I was thinking.

If something bad was on TV, I changed the channel. If I heard something disconcerting or if drama entered my world, I excused myself from it. I either looked for something good or positive, and if I was at home, I simply walked outside to my beautiful back yard and breathed in the glory that surrounded me. My outlook on life was in need of modification and staying connected to the *bad* wasn't something I was willing to do anymore.

Besides, if the Universe was listening to all of my thoughts, then I wanted them to be happy ones full of pleasant dreams. If that meant removing myself from people, places, and things, in order to accomplish my new harmonious lifestyle—consider it done.

As the two worlds continued to collide in my awake state, it became easier to soar into the new heights of mystery and into our new relationship as time passed. I knew a secret, so I thought, and a very special one at that. Diving into the deepest realms of each visitation dream while searching for *its* message was electrifying.

They were all amazing and many of them were very comforting. A few were especially easy to understand needing no deciphering skills whatsoever. But sometimes, there were those one-of-a-kind visits where Chip left me hanging with my mouth wide open. Like this one, where he decided to be *naked*.

As my eyes inched open, I saw my hands holding onto a black steering wheel. Slowly, my senses were coming together and the realization was quick — I was driving our Acura and Chip was sitting beside me in the passenger seat. I felt him there and at the same time, I recognized the road; Four Acre.

"Oh, we're taking him home and dropping him off," I presumed. I wasn't a happy girl. I felt the irritation creeping up inside. It was Friday night and Chip wasn't staying over. The disappointment and sadness was filling up my thoughts because I selfishly wanted him to myself.

I didn't get it either. He didn't have a good reason for breaking our routine. And then, I must have blacked out, because all of a sudden it was five o'clock the next morning.

I had driven back to Chip's house, not to stay of course, but to drop something off for him that he asked for. It was a computer-like object, but I knew it wasn't his computer.

As I walked up his driveway and set the item down on the porch, I glanced up. His bedroom light, as well as the living room one, was lit. The nosy me decided to take a peek inside.

I opened the front door slightly when I saw two young boys. They were both dressed in white underwear and were holding extra-large white bowls, eating cereal. One boy was about eight years old and the other around five or six.

A little further into the house was Chip. He was sitting on the corner of his couch, also holding a white bowl that was much larger than the boys', and eating cereal, too. Wrapped around him was a baby blue robe that was strikingly beautiful. Momentarily, I got stuck in the awe of its glow.

I gathered my senses quickly when the instant fear of getting caught, set in. I closed the door and speedily walked away. But then I heard it open behind me and I just had to see if it was Chip.

The older boy was standing in the doorway and was asking a question. My guilty conscience was rocking off the charts and my ability to listen had gone fuzzy. I couldn't hear anything he was saying.

"I'm just looking for Chip," I told him.

"Come inside, Lyn," the boy responded. "He's been waiting for you."

The door was wide open, waiting for my entrance. Slowly, I stepped inside when out of nowhere, darkness covered me.

When light re-appeared and my consciousness returned, I

was standing behind Chip. It was clear as day—I was staring at his back eyeing his new Tommy Bahama shirt, the one we purchased on vacation in the Florida Keys.

Oddly enough, he was picking up clothes out of a laundry basket on the bed, folding them nicely one-by-one, and placing each item in a very neat pile. He was very meticulous, handling each garment as though it might break. And me? I stood there watching, not saying a word, just enjoying being next to him.

Wanting to see what pants he was wearing, I then looked down. I had no idea the surprise that was waiting for me—he had nothing on from the waist down and his butt was staring at me, shining brightly. I burst into laughter. I couldn't help it.

He unhurriedly left the room, laughing too, while I gathered myself up and started a search for a blouse to wear— we were heading out that evening. I walked over to the closet and opened the door. There were only a few items of clothing hanging, nothing to speak of and nothing I cared to wear. When I went back to the basket on the bed, the basket was gone. And the clothes were missing, too.

"I don't remember seeing him move the clothes," I whispered. But then when I turned to look behind me, I saw them lying across the dresser, now unfolded.

"This is so not the Chip I know," I said. "He'd never do this to our clothes." I fumbled through and found the shirt I wanted.

...and then...

I took a walk outside to find his mom and join her on the patio. She was browsing through a photo album when she came across a picture of a house they once lived in. She began to explain the details of their home as I focused on two high-back chairs and a glass table inside the picture. The table was located on a porch sitting very low to the ground and as I glanced to the left of the photo, I noticed several puppies sprawled out. They were so cute.

Suddenly, one of them started to move inside the picture. I held the photo up higher, closer to my eyes, and watched the puppy's movement. He was crawling up a fence, straddling it, wiggling his tiny butt all around. His little back paws were shaking, kicking all about, and trying with all his might to get over the fence. Finally, he made contact and over and he went, falling to the ground. At the exact moment he leaped over, all the other puppies started to move around, too.

Astonished, I was amazed at their playfulness within the picture. Within the very image that sat between my fingers. I kept watching them play, ignoring everything else around me.

And then it hit me...

"Oh no," I said. "I have to get back inside before Chip questions why I'm messing around, not ready to leave."

I jumped up, excused myself, and ran into the house. When I entered the front door, I heard water running; Chip was in the shower. Approaching the bathroom, I stuck my head around the corner.

"You're in the shower without me?" I hollered.

The curtain moved as his face peeked out; he was carrying a huge smile. I took a couple of steps toward him as I watched him move the curtain to the side. He knew what I wanted to do; to kiss him.

To my sudden horror, water splashed me in the face. And then it hit me on the top of the head, and then my chest. I screamed bloody loud and at the same time, laughed so hard I almost peed. I yelled for Chip to stop and tried to duck out of the way. But he proceeded to step out of the shower and follow me with the nozzle.

I backed up into a corner, but he was still on my heels,

soaking me. While screaming at the top of my lungs, I finally collapsed into a ball, laughing until I cried as he drenched me more.

I couldn't escape him and I was now exhausted. Breathing hard and gasping for air, I felt the water finally stop. When I raised my head to steal a look, Chip was standing in front of me, naked as a jaybird.

He just stood there, sopping wet from head to toe, holding the nozzle in one hand, and laughing hysterically. He appeared quite proud of himself for soaking me.

Suddenly, my eyes shot open. I was frozen in bed, wide awake. Twirling my head to the other side, I searched for Chip, knowing he was there.

But he wasn't.

In the deafening silence, I revisited the movie-like dream more than once. Chip's ability to take me on such incredible and visual adventures warmed my heart. I was thrilled he was keeping us together, keeping us involved, alive, and making all of these wonderful new memories.

It was happening in a new arena, I got that, but it wasn't any different than before. Not really.

The more I thought about it, the more I remembered how Chip loved to be naked. It became just a thing when he was here in the physical world, so I didn't really think of it as being odd or strange. But looking back now, if Chip could have gotten away with it, he would have been happy being nude all of the time. Visualizing him standing there with no clothes, soaking wet, I couldn't help but be reminded of something he did not so long ago.

Headed for the Keys on vacation, we strategically planned our travels. We had decided to stop in and spend one night with my sister who lived in Fort Lauderdale at the time.

After spending a wonderful day together, it was time for bed. My sister housed us in her spare bedroom and from past visits, I knew it to be *the* hot room. For whatever reason, her venting system didn't keep this room cool. Prior to us arriving, she installed a new ceiling fan and it helped some, but it was still very warm.

Because we had such a good time, the next morning Chip asked if I'd like to stay an extra night, suggesting we head for the Keys the following morning. Of course, I wanted to stay. So I changed our reservations and we planned to check out the beach and drive down to Miami.

Everyone left the house early and then I started a search for Chip. When I found him, he had already shed his boxer shorts and was standing in front of me completely naked.

"If we're staying another night, we have to fix her venting system," he said. "I was miserable last night."

I followed him out to the garage, staring at his naked butt, while he searched for a ladder. The filter system was located in the ceiling.

He found the filters and then stated he needed me to hold the ladder in place as he climbed up. Before we did that however, he disappeared into our bedroom. When he returned, I noticed he was wearing something new.

"Why are you wearing shoes?" I asked.

Staring into my eyes without a smirk, without a smile, he seriously said, "The steps will hurt my feet." He lifted one bare foot and rubbed it, pouting.

"I need all the support I can get for my tender feet," he said. Because he said it so pathetically, I started to laugh. But when he looked up with a puzzled expression, I had to stop.

"Are you laughing at me?" he asked.

I couldn't tell if he was playing or not. Chip was very good at disguising his serious self-versus his playful self. I nodded my head *no* and chuckled, removed my eyes from his, and directed my attention back to the ladder. I grabbed it tightly as he positioned himself to climb.

I tried hard not to stare at his unclothed body because truthfully, it wasn't something I wanted to see. When he reached the top, the ladder started to wobble.

"Hold the ladder, darlin'," he said loudly but gently. "I don't feel like falling today." I grabbed it tighter, making sure it didn't move. And then I made a huge mistake. I looked up.

Oh my eyes… my poor, poor eyes. They were in shock. Complete and utter distress. All I could see was a small round butt squatting right in front me; I rapidly looked away. It was then that it hit me. My man was on top of the ladder butt naked.

Oh dear God, why did I look up?

I couldn't control myself as I burst into laughter. It was just so darn funny. Chip was mumbling something, asking for my help maybe… I don't know. I couldn't make heads or tails out of anything because I was laughing too hard.

I looked up again and just as I did, he lifted his right foot up to the next step, and now, all of his private parts were staring me in the face. I lost it. I lost all control. I was laughing so hard and so loud, tears fogged my vision.

Managing somehow to keep the ladder in place during my unforgiving cackling, I heard him laughing, too. Chip was much better at working through his giggling fit though. He changed the filter, handed me the old one, and then started his climb down.

I tried to get out of his way, but I didn't quite make it. Instead of waiting for me to move, he placed his naked butt smack dab on top of my head and wiggled it all around.

Yes, my sweetheart loved to be naked, and obviously, he

still did. It didn't take too long to start wondering if being nude within a dream carried any kind of symbolism. I heard this in a dream once; *symbols are the language of dreams.*

A symbol can invoke a feeling or an idea and often have a much deeper meaning than any one word could convey. At the same time, some symbols can leave the dreamer very confused. If you're like me, I pondered my dreams and wondered for days what they were all about. Hence my pull to ask for lots of guidance.

Interpreting my own dreams was a powerful tool. When analyzing them myself, I knew I should be able to learn about my deepest secrets and hidden feelings. Besides, no one was a better expert at interpreting my dreams than me. Starting out however, I saw no problem asking for help.

What is a dream-visit?

A visitation dream is the experience of our deceased loved ones visiting us while we sleep. This could be in the form of an in-person visitation, a verbal message, a sensation, or even through a pet, an animal, or other forms such as angelic Beings and invisible voices.

Dream-visits are different than a regular dream and often the dreamer notices this either during the dream itself, or upon waking. These dreams will be very real-like. The dreamer is much more aware and able to clearly remember the events that unfolded.

According to an article I once read, many people reported healing effects after having experienced a visitation dream. Especially if they needed comfort or were possibly questioning their faith. I got that. For me, Chip's visits gave me great comfort that he was indeed okay.

Have you experienced a visit from a deceased loved one?

Did it feel as real as us sitting here right now? If so, consider yourself very blessed. You have received a beautiful blessing; a special *kiss* from the *other side.*

Through my research, I learned of a few symbols that were common in dream-visits:

Death—death is a rebirth symbol. This is a sign of the transformation process. If you see your loved one dying, it's only to show you they've made the transition from the physical life to the Afterlife. Look at it like the life of a butterfly. A butterfly begins its life as a caterpillar. That caterpillar then turns into a beautiful butterfly after completing its life cycle and transformation. We too are like the butterfly. We move from the human form into the spirit form, but only after we shed our physical bodies. Death isn't bad; it's a new beginning.

Water—water is a healing symbol. If you see water in a dream-visit, this is a sign you are receiving healing energies from the other side and/or from your loved one. It can also signify our loved ones level of transition in the Afterlife. i.e.; blue water, white water, dirty water, dark water, clear water, etc. Each type of water may symbolize their growth, or yours.

Animals—totem symbols. If you see an animal in a dream-visit, it is a symbol. The best source for totem symbolism is a book by Ted Andrews titled, *Animal Speak.* Each animal embodies a particular energy that's been given to you. The easiest way is to look up the animal totem, even online but search for a spiritual definition, to understand the *message* being given to you. This also includes insects, birds, snakes, fish, etc.

Birth of a baby—creation symbol. If you see a baby born, if you are pregnant in a dream, or if you see someone close to you with child, all within a dream-visit, this too is a symbol. There are many explanations given online pertaining to a birth within a dream. For me, the baby dreams turned out to be part of a process to create something physical.

For example: I was given seeds on two separate occasions, handed to me in a dream by Chip. Each time he handed me these seeds, I wound up writing a book. I didn't put it together until four years later when he brought a child with him. The message was clear. Write a book for a child. So I did.

Birth of a baby or to be pregnant in a dream means to bring that dream into the physical world and create something new. It's a new beginning, the birth of something new.

I learned that when discerning a dream, the easiest way for me was to pretend I was explaining it to a three-year old child. This enabled me to put it in its most simplest form. Dreams are puzzles, no doubt, but they're also there to give us information, to give us hope, to give us a different way to look at life, and sometimes we can use those dreams for our creative endeavors.

Eleanor Roosevelt said it best. *"The future belongs to those who believe in the beauty of their dreams."* I don't know if she meant this in the context I suggest, but I like to think so.

We should believe in what we see within our dreams. We should learn from that content and then bring it forward and use the information within our physical world. When we believe in the beauty of our dreams, we can then see how stunning they really are.

To be naked in a dream, or to see someone nude in a dream... is to be free. It symbolizes freedom of all restrictions.

To see Chip naked was to see *all* of him. He had nothing to hide.

Chapter Twelve

I Love You

I looked forward to the weekends again. It took many months to get to that point, but when it arrived, I enjoyed using the time for peace and quiet and a reprieve from my over-stimulated mind.

Work was stressful—the only thing I looked forward to were my visits with Chip. My only task for this one particular weekend was to get Scooby over to the bath shop. It didn't matter if I accomplished anything else or not.

On Saturday morning, I did just that. I dropped him off at Amanda's, his bather, and then scooted across the street to K-mart to shop. This was pretty big for me because normally I made a straight line to the house and cocooned myself there.

My home became my prison. But it was one that carried a safety net to privacy. It was where I felt comfortable and could cry when I needed to. Where I could talk to Chip anytime I wanted without worry of someone seeing or hearing me. It was where I could sleep the day away if despair took me over, and it was where I learned to survive those months of misery alone.

Yes, this was very big for me.

Chip had bought a bunch of poinsettias at Christmas and they were starting to outgrow their present planters. Surprisingly, they had made it several months without a lot of attention from me. What I wanted to do was to put them into a large flower pot and give them room to grow.

After locating a new planter and fresh dirt, I paid for my goods and then exited through the garden center. As I walked toward my car, I sensed something trying to grab my attention. It was the sound of a melodious tune whisking through my thoughts as I faintly listened to the words: *Knights in white satin, never reaching the end.* It repeated a few more times like a record player, just those words, while I unpacked my buggy and placed the merchandise into the back seat.

I didn't really pay too much attention to the interruption. Instead, I focused more on my task at hand. I certainly remembered the song, but rather than thinking about it, I filled my head with a to-do list for later. For whatever reason, I ignored the song as I continued my descent down Normandy Boulevard.

For the first time since Chip had died, I decided to make a right-hand turn into McDonald's. I can't even count the mornings we pulled in to get *breakfast on the go* before we headed off to hunt for our house; a sandwich and tea were always needed.

I waited patiently in line at the drive-thru reading the menu. Just as I knew I would be, I was reminded of our visits while I pictured Chip sitting in the driver's seat and me over on the passenger side.

Even though Chip ordered the same thing every time, he'd sit for several minutes studying the menu. That drove me crazy. After he was done he'd bounce his head inside the car and say, "Same thing, baby doll?" I would nod my head *yes* and then he'd turn back and tell the attendant, "Give me two sausage, egg, and cheese McMuffins please. Give me one sweet tea and one unsweet tea, too."

Every time, without fail, he'd get back inside and say, "And they better get my tea right this time, damn it."

Immediate sorrow overtook me and I launched into a miserable cry. *God I miss him so badly!* I couldn't stop the waterfall from plummeting. The only thing I wanted more than anything in the world was for him to be back here with me.

Out of nowhere, an explosion of words invaded my crying thoughts. With perfect clarity, the melody and continued words to that song I heard moments earlier, was literally screaming at me now.

"Yes, I love you! Oh, how I love you!"

My head jerked back and my mind… well it shut itself up. I sat in shock. Momentarily, the sea of tears had been turned off because I couldn't believe what I had heard.

"Did I just make this up?" I asked myself. But before I could answer, it was my turn to order. Afterwards, I moved up one car length when suddenly, I was blasted again.

"Oh, how I love you!"

I then shouted, "I'm not making this up. I can hear you, Chip. I can hear you, loud and clear." My voice sailed through the car with extreme delight.

"I can hear you. Oh, my God, I can really hear you."

I paid for my order and listened to the song play in my head all the way home. But when I pulled into the driveway, the to-do list I made earlier bounced back in. Putting myself in *accomplish this-n-that* mode, the song repetitively played in the background of my thoughts while I transplanted the poinsettias. An hour later I finally gave in and walked into the house.

On the internet, I pulled up Google and typed, *Knights in White Satin*. The only thing that came back was a group called *The Moody Blues* linked to a song titled, *Nights in White Satin*. I quickly questioned myself as to why I had spelled it wrong.

After pulling up the song on YouTube and listening to its entirety, I sat and cried for a solid hour. I missed him. I loved him. I needed him. But that wasn't why I bawled today. What this was is beyond words and even at the time, my own comprehension.

What I experienced was love. Yet, this wasn't the same kind of love Chip gave me when he was here physically. This was a new love, a deeper love, a much different kind of love that was unlike anything encountered before. Yes, today I was more loved than ever and definitely not forgotten.

My sweetheart had found a way to *physically* say to me, "I Love You," while he lived in this different dimension.

Later that afternoon, I imagined something new. I asked myself, "What if I was them, souls in the Afterlife, and these were the words I used to convey a message? A message to my loved one I left behind."

It's quite beautiful:

~ Just what you want to be, you will be in the end. And I love you. Yes, I love you. Oh, how I love you! ~

What if our Loved Ones, our Angels, our Spirit Guides, our Universe that's filled with this beautiful and magical energy, what if they are our knights in white satin?

No ghosts ... only *Knights* ... in White Satin ...

Chapter Thirteen

Apport

Definition of Apport:
- a) The production of objects by apparent supernatural means; b) The objects produced.
- Spirituality, New Age, Astrology and Self-help/Alternative Belief Systems.

"About a month or so ago, I found a seed in my bathroom sink," I told Megan. "A little speck of something dark against something white."

"I was preparing for work one morning when I glanced down at this strange looking seed sitting in my sink. I stood there for a minute contemplating whether or not to pick it up."

"I did. The nosy me couldn't help it. I studied it for the longest time, rolling it around between my fingers, not fully grasping why or what it was exactly. It looked like a marijuana seed. When I acknowledged it as being so, I actually found myself laughing and instantly placed it up on the counter where I could see it every day."

"I knew it didn't get there all by itself. And since I live

alone, it wasn't possible someone else plopped a seed down in the sink. I like to think of it as a little gift from Chip from some far, far away land. I don't care that it's a seed. I only care that it's from him and that he's able to do something like this," I shared.

"More presents," Megan exclaimed. "A Mary Jane seed, that's so funny."

"I know, right? Well, about a week later, another seed appeared. This one sat on the corner of the sink and stuck out like a sore thumb. I picked it up to study it, but this time I heard the words *poppy seed* in my head. I relished in the excitement and laughed again, and then placed it on the counter next to the first one. They became my everyday reminder of how alone I am not."

"So then, my sister came to visit me. Excitedly, I showed the seeds to her and she too thought they looked like Mary Jane seeds. However, while she was getting ready one morning, one of them disappeared. She must have bumped it somehow with her tons of makeup bottles and creams (love you sister) and it slipped down the sink. I don't know for sure. I was a little upset and discouraged, but learning what I have these past months, I knew I had to let the gloom go and sadly, the seed, too. Whoosh, upset feelings washed away."

"And then… while I was getting ready for work yesterday, I thought about the seeds and silently wished for Chip to give me another someday. I told him I didn't care what kind they were—they were from him and that alone made them worth everything. So, this morning, I walk into the bathroom and much to my surprise, guess what sits on the counter next to the sink? Yes! Another seed. I'm so happy today. I'm on cloud nine. Neat stuff, huh?"

I was a tad frightened to share this story with Megan to

start out with. It was a little far out there. Seriously, how was someone else supposed to believe this happened just because I said it did? I knew how crazy it sounded. Trust me, I was skeptical as well, but it happened and I couldn't deny it. Heck, I had the darn seeds to show for it.

I do believe the Afterlife is capable of doing so much more than can be imagined. They, our loved ones, are the ultimate definition of Divine Magic. They know when we need a boost to lift our spirits and they know when we need a shoulder to cry on. They have the ability to choreograph and create the most amazing dreams and instill them into our unconscious thoughts while we sleep. They know the exact moment we need to hear, *I love you*. They are truly magically divine.

I don't know how Chip did some of the things he did; quite honestly, I stopped thinking about the *how*. All I knew was that when he shared a gift, it was heavenly and I was very happy when I saw it, heard it, or felt it, whatever *it* wound up being. I was and am very grateful and I feel extremely blessed. Not only to have had him in my life in the physical, but to have him in my life, even after death… it's extraordinary.

As for the seeds, the act of sending something from the other side to this side; the act of *apporting*, that was nothing I ever imagined could happen.

I asked Megan, "Why seeds in the bathroom?"

She said, "He's not just sending butterflies and using Scooby's snot to draw pictures on your windshield, he's sending actual items. Way cool. And, in the bathroom, with all of your bathroom dreams—that's powerful. You have enough energy, and so does he, to send you things, actual physical things. That isn't common anymore. There is more to learn and experience for you. This adventure is only beginning."

Little black seeds; my gems of joy. Chip may not be in his

physical form anymore, but he still had a thing for giving me gifts. His presents were exquisite and he had given me a total of three seeds. I thought about shipping one of them to Megan. We were very curious to learn what might happen if she held it and see if she could make out what it was. I had no idea at the time that I was in for a bombshell.

My phone rang early in the afternoon.

"Lyn, there are lots of images flashing by. Please tell me what makes sense, okay? First, I hear, 'test, test, test. Are you testing me again?' Okay, now I see clouds. Chip is flying through the clouds very fast. He has a goofy grin. Now I see a pair of jeans; tight or wet jeans around the knees. I hear, 'Hollow, like me.' Now I'm in a field with tall grass, sunflowers and trees, and Chip is rolling around in the field."

"I'm hearing, 'against all odds; write.' I see a pencil, a pencil tip, something is being inserted into the tip of the pencil; it's phallic. Chip has a goofy grin again and now he's performing acrobatics in the air saying, 'no gravity'. He says, 'write, write, write.' Now I see lines on a chalkboard. I'm reading, 'teach; penmanship; practicing penmanship.' He says, 'not as a punishment, but a way to communicate.'"

"He has an ear horn to his ear now. He says, 'place citrus slices over your eyes to see.' He's holding a bouquet of flowers for you. They're yellow, blue, purple, orange, and green. They're beautiful. Now I see a TV screen. I see you watching the screen looking for him inside of it, but he's not in the television—he's sitting beside you. He says, 'hatched. Hollow seed has hatched like a chicken."

She took a deep breath.

"The flashes are slowing down," she said. "I think that's it."

I was speechless. That was a lot of information to transmit

in such a short period of time, and all because of one tiny seed.

"Holy cow, Megan, that was exciting! But what do you suppose it all meant?"

"I think the testing is the image of filling in little circles, like the standardized tests in school," she said. "Chip flying through the clouds fast is his way of getting to you. His goofy grin proves how much he's enjoying all of this."

"The wet and tight jeans might have to do with his knees; they bothered him, right?" she asked.

"Yes, they did," I told her.

"His question, *hollow, like me?*, I have no idea," Megan said. "Have you made a mention of feeling hollow?"

"Yes, I have," I answered. "To be perfectly honest, that's exactly how I feel. I'm hollow inside."

"He understands how you're feeling," she explained. "Okay, the field with tall grass and sunflowers, rolling in the field, against all odds; that symbolizes the two of you, over there, making out in a field. Neat, huh?"

"That's hilarious," I laughed.

"Write, pencil, pencil tip; there were lots of writing references," she said. "Insert something into the tip of the pencil; Chip is the tip or the lead and you are the mechanical pencil. He's writing through you. The phallic reference? The seed struck me as kind of phallic."

(The definition of phallic means to represent something else by association. A material object used to represent something invisible.)

"The acrobatics in the air, no gravity; he has no knee problems now and he can do whatever he wants. More writing references; it's evident he wants you to write. The lines on a chalkboard is you, teaching. The penmanship reference is about practicing, knowing he's with you. Don't worry about grammar, he's with you. It's not a punishment because this is another way for him to communicate with you through your writing."

"The ear to horn; you're developing your clairaudience. When he said place citrus slices over your eyes to see, this is you developing your sight. The beautiful bouquet of flowers is a gift for you. Yellow flowers symbolize power. Blue is communication. Purple is sight. Orange is sex and emotions, and green is love."

"Every time you search for him in the TV, he's next to you instead, sitting beside you. The hatched, hollow seed; this is a big one. Chicken Little, maybe references to the panic of the world. The sky is falling, the sky is falling. How's that?"

"Oh my gosh, Megan, this has been amazing. Thank you so much."

There were two seeds remaining and every morning, I gazed at them in awe. I marveled not only at their travel, but also about their message, where they came from, what they were, and why they were there.

Yet, sometimes, none of that even mattered.

What mattered the most was… they were there.

Chapter Fourteen

Mastermind
with Joanne Gerber

B efore I found Megan and before I attended events of Sylvia Browne and John Edwards in 2008, I searched every day to find someone to assist me with my many dreams. I thought I truly needed someone to help me connect with Chip on the other side.

It was all I could think about. I was always in a mad-dash-mode to find a way to connect. And then, one day, I stumbled upon a website that belonged to Joanne Gerber.

Per the instructions, I e-mailed her to set up an appointment for a reading. Everything I searched through seemed perfect regarding her abilities to communicate with the deceased. I needed to find a way to talk to Chip and she felt like a good first step.

But when it came time to talk with Joanne, I was devastated. Her schedule was twelve months out and I had to make an appointment for the following year.

During 2008, many things changed and my insistent need for communication had subsided. It took several months to figure it out ... Chip and I were communicating through music. However, when I found a piece of paper in December reminding me of my upcoming scheduled reading with Joanne, I was delighted.

On January 13th, I found a quiet spot on a silent road to park in peace. I was excited, nervous, and my stomach felt full of butterflies. I couldn't wait to inhale any message from the man I still deeply loved and terribly missed.

Following is only part of the conversation. Many family members came forward first, some of which I identified afterwards. On a more selfish note, my Chip was the one I was waiting for.

Chip came forward and his murder was quickly acknowledged.

Joanne: Did he ever own a motorcycle?

Lyn: In his past, yes, but with us together, no.

Joanne: I don't know whether he has talked about it during your relationship that he wanted to buy a bike; I actually am seeing a Harley Davidson.

Lyn: Yes, ma'am.

Joanne: I thought that at one time he might have liked to put bikes together, or fix bikes, but he shows me a bike with tools on the floor. Like this is something he would have been doing.

Lyn: He wanted to buy a bike. Yes, he did.

Buying a motorcycle was not *on my priority list, but it was for him. He used to tease me, often, about getting me on the back of one of those rockets. I told him time and again if he bought one, he'd never get me to ride with him. "I seriously don't think that's going to happen, sweetie, and I don't know why you keep pushing for it." I told him once. He let me go on and on, just ripping into him and his insane idea while he sat*

144

there, laughing. After I was all done, he said, "Don't worry, baby doll, I would never put you in a situation that would harm you. Besides, I love watching you get all worked up."

His mom recently shared that his mode of transportation when he was stationed in Japan was a bike, a regular one, not motorized. He used to clean, grease, and check the tires all the time, pulling it a part and putting it back together. That would certainly explain the joy of taking a bike a part.

Joanne: Is there somebody with an Indiana connection?

Lyn: That's where my mother was born, I believe.

Joanne: Your mother was born there?

Lyn: Yes, I believe so.

Joanne: Okay. Like I said, everybody's still here, your grandmother, too. I think she wants to come back in, but I'm going to try to keep the connection. I feel like you want to make a connection with your fiancé. I want to try to keep that connection, okay?

Lyn: Okay.

Joanne: Interesting, what's with the tattoo? I don't know whether he was going to get a tattoo, or he has a tattoo?

Lyn: Actually, we were supposed to get a tattoo together and I just recently got one with Chip's name on my arm.

Joanne: On your arm—was it your left arm?

Lyn: No, it's my right arm. I do have one on my left arm though.

Joanne: So this was something you two were going to do before he passed?

Lyn: Yes, ma'am.

Joanne: So there was talk about it?

Lyn: Yes.

Joanne: Okay, so that's why he would be mentioning the
           tattoo. He shows me rolling up his left sleeve,
           he shows me rolling it up on his left arm. I felt
           either there was having one or talking about
           getting one when he was here. I just want to let
           you know he's bringing that through as
           validation.

Lyn: Okay, thank you.

*Chip wanted us to get a tattoo together; we actually talked
his mother into it, too. He wanted one on his left arm and no
matter the design, it was going to be something that symbolized
his love for the Florida Gators; I wanted a dolphin. What I
adored most about the plan was having it done together.*

Joanne: As I connect with his energy, I hear loud voices
           like an argument, and there was something with
           a fight.

Lyn: Okay.

Joanne: Do you understand this?

Lyn: I heard that afterwards, but I wouldn't put it past
           him.

Joanne: So you don't know what happened, what
           transpired before?

Lyn: Not between him and this man, no.

Joanne: Interesting, was Chip, I heard you call his
           name, so I'm going to call him Chip?

Lyn: Yes, ma'am.

Joanne: Was Chip also married before?

Lyn: Yes, once.

Joanne: Interesting, he keeps showing me a gold ring.
           So, I don't know if you have his ring, or there's
           a ring you have that belongs to him? Would

you understand the ring?

Lyn: Yes, ma'am. I bought him a gold ring for his birthday the year before last.

Joanne: Okay, so you have his gold ring?

Lyn: Yes, I do.

Joanne: Okay, thank you. He showed me that before, when he was first trying to come through, but he's bringing it through again, so I feel there's some sort of validation around that.

Lyn: Okay.

Joanne: I don't know whether you're wearing the ring or if you've thought about doing something with the ring, but there's definitely an acknowledgment about that.

Lyn: I have thought about reducing the size so I could wear it, yes.

Joanne: I think he would like that.

Lyn: Okay.

For me, when she asked if Chip had married before, it brought forth the marriage question between us. At my refusal to get married and my guilt for some of the things I had said about marriage, I believed this was his way of sending a gentle hint that we are married to each other, even if only in our hearts. The ring I bought him is merely icing on the cake and a reminder that he can see everything now. And she was right, only days before today, I picked his ring up and thought, "I think I'll have it resized so I can wear it."

Joanne: I really feel as I connect with his energy, a sense of regret. Like I feel there were a lot of things he needed to work out in this lifetime. I feel somebody who was very stressed. He had a lot of worries, maybe didn't really buckle down and take life as serious as he should have; do you understand?

Lyn: Yes, I do.

Joanne: And I feel like there are regrets with that, because I feel like he has left you in a position that he's feeling very badly about—the way he left here so suddenly and leaving you behind dealing with the situation. I really feel that even though he was tough on the outside, he was very sensitive on the inside.

Lyn: Very, very sensitive on the inside.

Joanne: Yeah, and I felt almost like, he might have been battling issues with low self-esteem, feeling he wasn't good enough for you. Do you understand?

Lyn: Yes, ma'am. I do.

Joanne: And I want to say he's very sad about this, and that you put up with it. He's saying, "She put up with me."

Lyn: (I laughed) I did. Yes, ma'am.

Joanne: He even told you that.

Lyn: Yes, ma'am.

Joanne: "She put up with all my," I can't swear, but it's S H. Do you understand what I'm saying?

Lyn: You can swear if you want to, but I do, yes.

Joanne: He says, "She put up with my shit."

Lyn: (I got such a charge out of that.) Yes, I did.

Boy, did I ever put up with his crap. I know I paint a pretty picture of him when I write about him, and I know he knows how much I love him, but truth be told, boys will be boys and he did get under my skin a time or two.

Joanne: I have to say that, because I validated you.

Lyn: Okay, thank you. Yes, that's him.

Joanne: Did he write you letters?

Lyn: No.

Joanne: Any notes that you have, left you a note on your car, some sort of letter or note?

Lyn: He did many years ago, but I can't find it. I don't know if I threw it away.

Joanne: You'll come across those when you're cleaning up. But he's showing me putting something on your windshield.

Lyn: No. Oh, he drew me pictures! (I was elated! I pounded my feet on the floor in utter joy.)

Joanne: Did he put it on your windshield?

Lyn: I have at least ten pictures that he's drawn since he died on my windshield.

Joanne: Okay, so that's what he's talking about? Pictures on the windshield?

Lyn: Yes, ma'am.

Joanne: All right, he's just letting you know that's him connecting. What do you mean pictures?

Lyn: He started by drawing fish; I have a butterfly, I have a squirrel, I have a clown face…

Joanne: Was this while he was here?

Lyn: No, this is after he died.

Joanne: On your windshield?

Lyn: Yes, on my windshield.

Joanne: Like with a mist, like with his fingers; something like that kind of drawing?

Lyn: I don't know how he did it, but they're there. I took pictures of them; I've got pictures of all of them.

Joanne: Oh, wow.

Lyn: I've had so much happen since he passed away.
          I knew they were from him, I just knew it.

Joanne: Okay, yes. I just have to tell you about putting
          something on your windshield because that's
          what he's showing me. Please take that as
          validation.

Lyn: Okay, thank you.

There's not a slim chance, not even a remote possibility, that Joanne could have known about the pictures on my windshield. At the time of this reading, 1-13-2009, I was still writing "Wake Me Up!" and it wasn't even close to being completed. As for the website where the pictures can now be viewed, it wasn't until the summer of 2009 before that site was even built. Only Megan and close family members knew about the pictures. This was a fantastic surprise, and a grand validation that he was the mastermind behind them all.

Joanne: I just feel that things are going to come through
          with all of this. I can feel that whatever
          happened, he might have gotten loud, he might
          have raised his voice to somebody, some sort of
          dispute; but I do feel they're going to find out
          who did this.

Lyn: They already know who did it, they just haven't
          arrested him.

Joanne: All right, he will be arrested. I do feel that.

Lyn: Do you know when? Can he tell you when?

Joanne: He's a pretty big guy, isn't he?

Lyn: Yes, he is.

Joanne: You know this guy?

Lyn: Yes, I do.

Joanne: He's been in trouble before.

Lyn: Yes, he has.

Joanne: I feel like this is somebody that might have a record or be a trouble maker.

Lyn: Yes, ma'am; he is.

Joanne: Yes. I'm sorry, your question was *when*?

Lyn: Yes.

Joanne: I don't know; I'm not really getting a sense of exactly when. But it might be in the next six months to a year.

Lyn: Okay.

Joanne: You know ... nobody loves you ... and I really feel that ... like I do. Do you say that when you talk to him?

Lyn: I tell him that all the time. Nobody loves you like I do.

I was bouncing up and down in my seat with this one and I had a smile clear across my face. Only Chip, no one else in the whole world could have known what I said to him in the privacy of my home. Every night, before sleep took me away, I told him I loved him. And I always added, "Nobody loves you like I do..."

Joanne: And I'm really sorry about how it all happened. I wish it ...

She stopped with this thought. Even though she never finished the sentence, I knew what the words were supposed to be. By this time, I knew what Chip was up to. I knew he was telling her things only I've said. With this one though, it came at a time when I was hurting bad and my heart was heavy with pain. What I said was, "I'm so sorry for how this happened to you, Chip. I wish it were me, my love, not you."

Joanne: He's so emotional. He can be very emotional, too.

Lyn: Oh, yes. He's my big loving teddy bear.

Joanne: Yeah, he was like a baby—you rescued him, he says.

Lyn: I've been told that, yep.

Joanne: You rescued—you tried to help him.

Lyn: I did.

Joanne: And a lot of times, he just didn't listen to you. And you were putting your energy out there; you did make a difference in his life. You changed his life around. You gave him a reason to live, I want to say. I don't know whether he ever tried committing suicide, or was depressed, but he's saying you gave him a reason to live.

Lyn: I remember him telling me, *you make me want to be a better man.* That's what he would say to me.

Joanne: Yeah, so know you have made a difference in his life, you helped him. I want to say you were like the Earth Angel in his life and he loves you.

Lyn: That's so sweet; I love him.

Joanne: He just gave me a peace sign.

Lyn: Yes, definitely. He's the peace man.

Joanne: So, know you have another validation from him to you.

Lyn: Thank you.

Every day I looked at pictures of him never putting two and two together. It was after this reading I realized I was wrong in thinking his peace sign was entirely about our Hawaii connection. His peace sign was in almost every picture of him throughout his life. It's what he did. He peaced out.

Joanne: I'm sorry about your loss.

Lyn: I just wish he were still here.

Joanne: I know. But know that he is watching over you like a guardian angel. And I think you have a good connection—and he loves music. He's showing me music.

Lyn: Yes, he gives me songs all the time.

Joanne: And you must listen to them, they remind you of him, because his connection to music is really shining.

Lyn: I do. He gives me the songs and I go look up the lyrics. Every one of them is a love song of some sort.

Joanne: To receive such validation and communication from him—he's a very strong communicator. And I want to say that when he was on the Earth plane, I bet if there was something on his mind, boy he'd let you know it.

Lyn: Yes, he did. (And boy did he ever.)

Joanne: Because those are the strongest communicators and I can tell he's a very strong communicator.

Lyn: Is there a reason why he's communicated with me so desperately this past year?

Joanne: I think you were open to it. I think you want to connect with him. I don't think it was necessarily out of desperation. I think you allowed it, which is a wonderful thing. You allowed your heart and mind to be open to a world that you might have been unsure exists. And he was trying to show you that he's okay, because he went very fast. It was very traumatic around his passing. And that he wanted to let you know. I think that was a strong message right there. I think because of the way he

	passed.
Lyn:	Okay.
Joanne:	Make sense?
Lyn:	Yes, it makes perfect sense.
Joanne:	What's most important is to acknowledge the validations, the evidence of Chip's survival, that he is around you. That's what's most important.

The evidence of Chip's survival... I fell in love with those few words. Once our reading ended and I had placed the phone down, a tremendous sigh of relief rushed in. I felt a huge amount of sadness, but at the same time, I also felt happy; almost skippy-like. I felt so blue, but even peaceful, too. All of the joy and delight in hearing from Chip again, raced through me at the same time as the sorrow of his disappearance. My body had no other alternative. It turned the raw emotions into stinging tears.

With a stream flowing across my face and my mind racing wildly in thought, I suddenly sensed him. In my mind's eye, I saw Chip standing in front of the car. He was wearing his navy blue sweat shirt, his arms were folded across his chest, his head was slightly tilted to the right, and he was smiling. He was very proud of himself; he was proud of *us*.

It then hit me—the day before this reading with Joanne, I made a promise to Chip. I was talking to myself, like I always did, and said something silly, out loud.

"If you can make Joanne say something personal, something only you and I know, then I'll promise to *believe*. I'll vow never to question our ability to communicate through my thoughts."

I imagined he replied, "You promise?"

And then I answered, "Yes, I do."

I heard him then say, "Consider it done."

When he said that, goose bumps covered my entire body and I knew right then that I shouldn't question the odd chills. But you know me... I questioned everything.

After this reading with Joanne though. I didn't anymore.

How could I?

Chapter Fifteen

Abracadabra

October 31st fell on a Sunday in 2010. It was a weekend filled with fresh promises and a new life about to begin. As exciting as it was to close on a new house in Georgia, I was covered with great sadness, too. The only home Chip and I shared was going be left behind soon, for good.

That Saturday brought with it of a great deal of work and shopping for materials. Arrangements were made to clean up the new abode with fresh paint and new carpet. Everything moved with such super-fast speed, it was hard to keep up.

Exhaustion set in that evening and the only thing desired was sleep. The ride back to Florida the next day was going to be a very long and tedious experience. A few weeks earlier, I had purchased a pickup truck and it, too, was waiting for me to drive back. I had never owned a truck. For that matter, I had never *driven* a truck before. Riding high up in the air made me a little apprehensive but more so, the fear of the truck taking up so much room on the highway scared me. Just the thought of it all had me feeling ill.

When I test drove the truck, I fell in love with its Cadillacstyle comfort ride. *Oh yeah,* I thought, *I can do this.* But there was one more thing to worry about—I decided to borrow my sister's pull trailer. For six or seven long hours, it was my belief I could drive a truck and pull a trailer, one that was wider than the truck itself, and somehow make it safely into the driveway of my home in Jacksonville. My plans were much larger than my reality and sleep didn't come easy.

The next day, the trailer was hooked up nice and tight and the truck was packed with my belongings. Scooby hopped up in the back seat with no problems and Angel snuggled up in her bed up front. It was time to get the show on the road.

We were off.

The first two hours in the Atlanta traffic was horrible. My body was so tense, my arms felt like heavy weights. My back ached so badly, no position was comfortable.

I was scared to death.

The trailer tires were merely inches from the lines and that was only if I kept the truck directly in the middle. Passing semis was a complete nightmare. My heart pounded fast, long before I reached the first set of their tires. And the traffic? Horrible, just horrible. Eight lanes of speeding cars all going the same way and all of them racing each other.

It was crazy insane.

Once we were out of Atlanta, the traffic slowed down and I felt more at ease. I was able to relax my tense body and was doing okay. We were half way home.

But then, out of nowhere, I remembered something.

"I forgot the key to my house," I shouted. "Oh no!"

I knew I couldn't very well turn around and go back to get it, I was too far away. *Call your sister*, I thought. So I did.

She checked the car to see if I left the key behind and indeed, I had. I then called my mom and asked if she still held a spare key but no, of course she didn't. Dummy me changed the locks some time ago and only I had the key.

"Well isn't this just grand?" I told myself.

There was no way to get inside the house. I knew it would be close to impossible to get a locksmith on a Sunday night, so I chose not to entertain that idea. The only thing I could imagine to do was break a window and then climb in.

"Yes," I convinced myself, "that's what I have to do. I'll repair the window tomorrow."

For the next hour I plotted which window to break, which one wouldn't be so expensive to repair and soon, I had devised the perfect plan. My safest bet was a small window to the living room on the back side of the house, inside the screened patio. I would find a screw driver in the Acura that was still parked in the driveway, I'd wrap a towel around my hand to protect it, and then stab the window to break it.

"Yes," I congratulated myself, "I've got it all figured out."

Another hour passed finding us somewhere around Tifton, Georgia. We had a couple more hours to go and I was getting very comfortable behind the wheel, feeling much more confident. I sat back in my seat and decided to enjoy the ride.

All thoughts of what was ahead quickly disappeared; they were gone. What did appear however, and quite apparent, were direct words to a song.

If only you believe like I believe baby, we'd get by, I heard.

I sat in shock. Disbelief no, but shock, yes. My thoughts returned to those words and when they did, I heard a bit more of the lyrics to the song.

If only you believe in miracles baby, so would I.

Goose bumps immediately climbed across my arms; I knew this was no accident. The words continued to repeat themselves over and over again.

"I know that song," I hollered, "I remember that song."

Of course, I didn't remember the artist or the band. I've never been good with names. I couldn't remember much more of the lyrics either, but I heard the tune of the song loud and clear in my head.

And then I got it. It was easy to recognize and understand.

I wasn't alone on my journey down the busy highway. My love, my Chip, my very best friend in the whole world, was right there with me.

Joy lifted me up, and happy crawled through my veins.

The hours flew by quickly. Merely two exits away and my gas gauge sat on *E*. I knew I wouldn't make it to the house. Certainly, I had hoped there'd be no veering off and maneuvering around a gas station with a trailer, but I had no choice. Gas was needed.

Luckily, I picked a great spot. It cost two cents more a gallon, but I was able to pull straight in and drive right out. I knew not how to back a trailer—I had to drive it forward. I did wonder though, *was I directed to that gas station?*

We had driven non-stop and my bladder was screaming. It was turning dark and I seriously didn't want to drive my beast with no daylight. I decided to wait.

"We're only ten minutes from the house," I told myself. "I can wait." Besides, it wasn't fair if I went and didn't allow the kids to go, too. We were almost home.

Yikes! Every inch of sidewalk and roadway was covered with parents and costumed children. As I turned into the neighborhood, it became apparent that today was a special day. Today was *Halloween.*

"Crap, I left my front porch light on," I said, out loud. "They're going to think we have candy."

All I could do was inch forward. It was taking *forever.*

When I finally reached my cul-de-sac, the commotion was even worse. There were so many people standing around, in the middle of the street, on the sidewalks, in the yards; the number of people—was absurd. I couldn't move at all.

"It's never been like this in the past," I mumbled.

My yard was only feet away and I wasn't allowed to drive in. I had to potty so bad. And Scooby, dear God, he wasn't making things any easier. He was jumping back and forth from window to window, barking loudly at each passerby. He was seriously pinching my very last nerve of the day.

Some ten minutes later, I pulled into the front yard. Until I practiced backing, the truck and trailer was fine right where she sat. It was really dark out. My first hurdle was helping Scooby hop from the truck. He was still excited and nothing I said stopped him from running his big mouth. He wasn't shy in the least either. I wanted us to be invisible and he wanted us to be seen. Scooby won.

After retrieving Angel from the passenger side and tucking her under my arm, we began our journey to the back yard. I still had to break into the house.

We stood in front of a barrier at the side gate that I built some time ago. My sweet Angel was a naughty little girl. She loved sneaking out whenever my back was turned and literally would disappear down the road. She must have thought she was made of steel, and believed that her twelve pound little body was tough enough to withstand anything, even the big dogs.

No joke, one time she ran up to a Rottweiler and began telling him off. That was all it took. She freaked me out. Bad! I just knew the Rottie was going to take one bite and she'd be gone forever. Instead, he surprisingly ran away with Angel chasing close behind. That very day, I built the barricade to keep her inside the yard.

Except now, I couldn't see the gate very well because it was so dark out. The chained knot wasn't coming loose and my irritation was growing by leaps and bounds. I continued to fight with it, but the slightest movement of my body was excruciatingly painful; I had to potty, bad.

Angel was squirming under my arm and Scooby was pulling on his leash from between my legs. The pain was really starting to affect my judgment, too. I wasn't screaming yet, but I was *very* close to the edge of losing it.

Suddenly, the gate just opened. Hallelujah. I was never so happy. After placing Angel on the ground and releasing the monster, I closed the gate behind us and began to walk up the small incline to the patio.

Glancing at the side of the house, I contemplated my task ahead, breaking in, and wondered if I could continue. I looked back at the patio only feet away now and watched Scooby enter the doorway. Alarmingly, he stood in place, barking like crazy while staring at the back door to the house.

Scooby was a very vocal boy, so I didn't give his loud bark much thought right away. I did, however, watch him leap forward and disappear into the darkness. Unexpectedly, Angel decided to join him. She left my side and raced up the steps.

Angel was an old gal and didn't move about too quickly. Witnessing her sudden burst of energy amazed me. When she hit the top step, Scooby re-appeared.

Standing in the doorway now, they both gawked into that twelve foot gap of darkness—each of them barking loudly— while I stood frozen several feet away. They had my full undivided attention.

I tried to focus into that dark gap of space and search for any kind of movement, but I saw nothing or anyone standing there. So I decided to take two steps forward.

The kids weren't letting up.

Scooby turned his head and looked me dead in the eyes. He was panting, smiling, and then he instantly turned his head back to look at the door in question. A very weird feeling began to grow.

Out of nowhere, a light suddenly appeared. It was shining on them both and slowly, it was getting brighter and brighter. The kids were getting much louder, too. Angel was jumping up and down in place, barking. Scooby was standing over her, wagging his tail wildly, shouting.

"Where is that light coming from?" I questioned.

Quickly, they both *leaped* out of view. Trying to keep Scooby's tail in sight, my eyes reached the door and shockingly, I watched it gradually creep open.

"What? The light's coming from inside the house?" I whispered. "But how?"

I started to tremble. Scooby's bark was more intense now.

Everything was moving fast... the kids... the light... the door opening... fear had suddenly grabbed me up and was squeezing the life right out of me. I froze! I couldn't breathe. All I could do was stand still, scared to budge.

"Oh no, someone's inside the house," my voice quivered, "and is stealing everything we own."

My bladder was screaming louder and right then, I knew I couldn't stand still another second. It was time to move.

"If someone's inside the house and it's our time to go," I determinedly said, "well, it's going to have to be our time, by God. I have to potty."

After reaching the top of the steps, the kids greeted me. They quickly turned away and ran into the house through the now *wide opened* door. I was very hesitant, but I tiptoed ahead.

I held onto the sides of the door and peeked in to see if anyone was in the living room. There was no one there.

Scooby was still howling.

To the left was the kitchen; Angel was drinking from her water bowl and big ole Scoober was standing over her, screaming at her to move. He wanted a drink, too, but Angel was hogging the water and loving every second of it. Her fast wagging tail spoke volumes.

"They don't seem to be sensing anything going on in here," I assumed. "Have they missed something?"

There was no one in the kitchen. To the right was the dining room, but no one was in there either. I grabbed the bat at front door and took a look around the living room again, making a special note that nothing seemed touched.

Holding the bat over my head, I inched down the lengthy hallway. My heart was beating hard and fast, getting a perfect workout. After opening all the doors and flipping on all the lights, I found no one in the house. The last room was my bedroom, but nothing there either. I ran to the bathroom.

After checking all the rooms again, even the closets and the garage, I found no one in the house. I walked back to the magical *opening-by-itself* door and suddenly realized the depth of the situation. I had help. None of that which took place happened all by itself.

Yes, I most certainly had assistance. Who was I to ignore the gifts the Afterlife could bestow upon me? Chip was amazing. Do I believe in miracles, as the song stated hours earlier?

Oh yeah! ~*Miracles*, by Jefferson Starship.~

I believe in miracles, baby!

Chapter Sixteen

Sacrifice
with Leslie Dutton

S ometimes I woke up feeling extremely tired. The dream world was incredible, but it was also very exhausting. Many times it felt like I traveled a thousand miles and then back, allowing no time to rest.

It was natural to question everything since nothing felt *normal*. This unusual journey was filled with multiple turns and discoveries and I was certain I hadn't signed up for any of it. Discerning dreams took a great deal of practice and required life experience. My interpretations were getting better, but not always with great success. Learning my personal symbols would later be one of my greatest feats.

Symbols are the language of dreams. Since I understood this, I oftentimes revisited an incredible dream that was a couple of years old. It made no sense at the time, but in 2011 a real-life opportunity to share it presented itself.

Through Facebook, Leslie entered my life. In time, her mediumship abilities revealed themselves and the topic of dreams arose in many of our conversations. One day, I found the courage to ask for her interpreting expertise. When she said *yes*, I was thrilled.

After printing it up, I started reading the dream to her:

Lyn: My immediate recollection placed me in a room inside of an enormous castle where I was surround by family. It was a present day celebration with relatives in this lifetime, but also with kin I knew very well from the other side, too.

Leslie: This shows where you were surrounded by people who loved you and supported you, Lyn. Some of them have been with you for many lifetimes.

Lyn: There were several people speaking at the same time. My head bounced from face to face, intently listening to their words.

They were saying things like; *it's what you know you have to do; we will always be here to support you; we're all here for you; we're so excited it's you; what an honor this is. He chose you, dear; yes, you have to. You know you do.*

Confusion bounced in and it grew larger, building on each comment. In the moment, I somehow knew exactly what it was I had to do. I knew I had to do this because *this* was what *He* wanted. I was so scared to do it, however, and I felt like *He* was much larger than any of us there.

Leslie: Yes! God, Spirit, Your Higher-Self... the Universe. You knew deep inside you had to go through with it, even though you didn't know what *it* was.

Lyn: Exactly! I knew I had to do it, Leslie, no matter what. And I knew it was what *He* wanted.

Okay... it was at that moment I turned and saw none other than Allison DuBois. Allison is an author and medium and her talents were formed as the basis of the TV series, *Medium*.

She was standing in front of me holding a book in her hands, studying it. She was flipping through the pages, focused on reading. I swore I felt like I had known her all of my life. Suddenly, she looked up from the book and gazed into my eyes.

She said, "Lyn, we don't have to tell you that this is what you need to do. You already know it is. The only thing you should remind yourself of—is *why* you've been chosen."

She then lowered her head and said, "And that's because of *His* love." Her voice was gentle and filled with kindness. I stared at her while she buried her eyes back into the book and returned to reading.

Leslie: Allison Dubois represents a woman who, through her dream state, is precognitive. This was the image you recognized; therefore, this was the image shown to you. And the fact that she was reading a book really says it all. She symbolized your dream state and you writing your book about your communications with Chip.

Lyn: Oh, my God, I never thought of it like that. That makes perfect sense, Leslie. Wow…

Okay… I was slowly accepting I had been chosen. My thoughts were filled with the nice compliments from family, and with Allison's reminder about why I needed to do this, too. It was hard, but I was sincerely trying to accept the celebration.

Suddenly, a pool of information filled my head. Out of nowhere, I understood it. I knew that on an exact moment in time, on an exact date in the future, I would do this for *Him*. The *it* wasn't mentioned though, so I kept asking myself, *What do I have to do?*

Leslie: The pool of information that filled your head— yes, this was the *knowing* being given to you. You began to search through books to make sense of it all and gain *the knowledge* in a format that only you could understand.

Lyn: I did that, exactly. That's so true. I love this! Okay, okay, where was I?

The silence took over the celebratory laughter and chatter. But somehow, my thoughts were being read; I could feel it. I was guided to lie on top of a flat surface—a very long and beautiful oak table. My brother Billy, who is deceased, was standing in front of me; he was there to share all of the answers and tell me what was going to happen.

Out of the blue, my body started to change. I wasn't the same person, yet I couldn't see how I looked; there were no mirrors. The reaction from everyone though—laughter, hollers, voicing excitement—told me I had already begun the stages of this bodily change. As I glanced at all the faces in the crowd surrounding me, I saw the proud smiles gazing down.

Leslie: Your body has indeed changed. You have a heightened awareness and an incredible ability to recall the messages you receive while in the dream state—right down to the last tiny detail.

Lyn: Back when I had this dream, Leslie, I think the awareness was more intense. Does that make sense?

Leslie: Absolutely!

Lyn: Okay…

My brother was standing beside me, chanting in an old English accent and slowly walking around the table.

"On the exact minute in time, on the exact date given, this sword,"—he lifted a beautiful, extremely bright and shiny sword up into the air—"this sword will be thrust into your heart, Lyn."

His wrist moved back and forth high above me, gallantly displaying its brightness to all who watched. The radiant shine sparkled on each side of its silver body, whence now I saw the enormity of its size. It was huge.

Billy said, "When this happens, Lyn, you will then have given yourself away to help the ones who need you."

Leslie: Okay, the Ceremonial Sword and Alter like table—to me the sword may represent a power that you will soon realize. To me, the sword may also represent victory when moving forward. Giving yourself away to those who need your help—you help people understand the transition process, death, and that receiving messages from departed loved ones is not only possible, it's natural.

You will be a teacher of many and an inspiration to all. Perhaps the sword is also symbolic of this inspiration. This inspiration has always lived inside your heart.

The heart stores the forever memories of the past, including past lives. This is about what your future in this life has in store for you, Lyn. I find it fascinating that you wrote this two years ago, and now you've made it happen.

Lyn: Wow, I didn't see any of that back then. Your words ring such truth; I'm covered in goose bumps.

All right, more…

Billy was towering over me with the bright sword yielding between his hands. I instantly saw the sacrifice I had to make… my life. Fear quickly kicked in as I whispered, "I don't know if this is something I can do. I don't want to feel that kind of pain. When that sword enters my heart, it will hurt really bad. I don't want to die."

As soon as I said that, voices echoed throughout the room with more good wishes. *What a blessing to have been the one chosen to rise up to this occasion and share it with so many; what an honor for you to be the one He chose; we are so very proud of you.*

Leslie: The sacrifice may indicate old beliefs falling away. Your former life falls away. Being in a state of pain after

Chip's death was truly sacrificial. It took you to a new place you never imagined you'd go. Had you not made this sacrifice, you would not have been able to relate to this new inspiration. The sacrifice is how they got your attention. And yes, you were indeed chosen, in my humble opinion.

Lyn: My attention was indeed grabbed, Leslie. I can see the sacrifice now; it *was* Chip dying and me surviving his death. That was indeed the most pain I've ever experienced.

Okay, where was I...

I then screamed, "But I don't want to die."

Leslie: This was fear of letting go of your old life and uneasiness about the new information that you would receive in the coming years.

Lyn: That's interesting. I think I still fight giving up my old life. Sometimes, I want it back...

I fled. Somehow I had gotten away and was hiding from everyone. As I looked around to identify my new surroundings, I noticed I was in a construction yard with large heavy equipment. I had located cover under an enormous crane. It was dark out and no one would find me there. "At least not for tonight," I said.

Leslie: The construction yard—construction, to me, represents building. You were indeed building a new life. The darkness—you were unclear and you hadn't quite seen *the light* yet.

Lyn: Oh, that makes perfect sense...

Instantly, I was in another person's body; I was a man, running fast and trying to flee the police.

Leslie: This is interesting, Lyn. This may be the old religious dogma that your spirit wanted to escape, manifesting into the image of *police*.

Lyn: That *is* interesting, and never occurred to me.

Inside the man, it was quite evident I had no desire of being caught. As I ran, I noticed a construction yard ahead, so I leaped on top of a telephone pole to get a better look. I then jumped across them, high up in the air like Superman, flying from one pole to another.

Unexpectedly, a large bull dozer in the construction site appeared and I jumped down on top of it. After climbing to its empty bucket, I soared inside and wiggled the power lines, hard. The bucket then released and unexpectedly, it dumped me out on top of a large pile of sand.

The sirens were getting louder in the distance and I knew I had to hide, quickly. Roaming fast across the yard, I considered refuge under a large crane.

Leslie: The construction versus the police—this is your spirit yearning for this new structure of belief, your true self, yet the old dogmatic attitudes still chase your soul. You morphed into a *body* that may be, in your mind, unrecognizable to the police in an attempt to disguise yourself.

Lyn: I was back to me again, Lyn, and still hiding underneath the enormous crane. My eyes were glued to a strange man who appeared out of nowhere. From the moment he dumped himself out of a bucket and landed flat on his back, I'd watched his every move.

He was running from the law; the sirens were loud. Of all things, he was wearing a white tee-shirt making him stand out like a sore thumb. "What a bozo," I said, out loud. "I hope he runs the other way."

My eyes were glued to him. But when he looked in my direction, I swore he saw me, so I leaped back. I then quietly pleaded, "No! Please don't come over here."

Burying my head in my lap and trying to squeeze closer to the large tire, I was hoping he'd go away. Suddenly, I sensed his presence and could feel him very close. When I looked around the tire again, he was squatting in front of me. He turned to peek around the corner to see if anyone had noticed him, and then came back to meet my eyes. His voice then pierced my ears.

"There you are," he said.

Leslie: This man could have been a soul looking for a kindred spirit. One who would understand him. And he found you.

Lyn: "You have to go away," I shouted. "Right now! Just go!" The sirens were closer. The reflection of their lights were bouncing inside of his eyes.

The grounds filled with police, they were everywhere. One car came to a halt only feet away and then shined flood lights directly on me. Just like that, as bright as the day itself, I could be seen hiding under the crane.

"I have no choice now," I told myself. "I have to go back and do what it is I know I'm supposed to do."

Leslie: Yes! Here is where your soul made the decision to *come out* of the spiritual closet, so to speak, and face the naysayers.

Lyn: I can totally see that now, wow…

As I slowly walked beside this guy toward the police car, I loudly professed, *"When this man was found, so too, was I."*

In an instant, my eyes bolted open. I was lying flat on my back and staring straight up at the ceiling. I shot up on my elbows looking for the kids—they were fast asleep at the foot of the bed. I collapsed in mystery, unable to grasp what I had just experienced. I rolled over to look at the clock and in its mystical blue shadow, it showed, 11:11.

Leslie: Forget for a second that many believe eleven is a key spiritual number. Look at the shape of those numbers—

11:11—they appear to be pillars, a gateway, two dots, one atop of the other. Two enlightened spirits connected, you and Chip.

The elevens on your clock, too, are a message that this will all be in full fruition mode around that time. 11/11.

To think I sat on this dream-visit for two years, never asking anyone about its message, was nothing short of a beautiful sign. Leslie made it all come back to life, turning the dream into a reality that made perfect sense. Not only did I understand the visit afterwards, I also realized how important *symbols* were.

Symbols are the language of dreams.

The celebration of family and very dear friends; my deceased brother showing me my sacrifice; the sword that would change my heart forever; Allison Dubois reading my book... I could see it so clearly now.

My sacrifice was losing Chip. His job was to wake me up. Together, we would write a book about communicating through space and time, as well as sharing his work in the Afterlife. It was all true, I sacrificed the life I had always known and stepped into something I knew absolutely nothing about.

In my humble opinion, Chip sacrificed much more than I. He gave up his life so I could be awakened to what else exists after the physical world.

I once desired to know everything there was about the Afterlife and the Universe. Now, not so much. The mystery of life would be ruined. The tests of life would be no more. The beauty of life, forever gone.

What I love most about life today... having given up controlling it.

Chapter Seventeen

Physicality
with Colleen West

My entire body jerked. My heart was racing fast, from fear, and my chest felt like it was about to explode. Her voice was screaming inside my head, still.

"Help me! Someone, please help me!"

Wide awake and cringing with fright, I was lying safely in my bed, but freaking out. "Was she real?" I questioned. "Or did I make her up?" It took another second or two before the light bulb moment kicked in.

"Oh, my God! She was real!" I shouted.

There were buckets piled everywhere across the floor. A male's voice had already informed me that massive amounts of chemicals were being dumped into the ocean, every day. This man was guiding me through a large plant, showing the chemicals they had confiscated.

He described how they collected the illegal toxins from oil companies such as, Exxon, BP, Shell, and many more. They then tested the chemicals and fined the oil companies based on the limit of deadly toxins found.

There were many types of toxic substances revealed. Some were exposed in powder forms, many were liquids, and even a large quantity was hidden in round concrete bench weights. And then outside, standing next to the water, the guide pointed in the opposite direction.

He said, "Over there by the house on the hill, lies more of the powder substance. You can see it all along the fence line."

As I looked through and then over the fence, I couldn't see a house anywhere. All I noticed were hills of sand. I must be too short to see over the fence, I told myself.

Just as that thought crossed my mind and my eyes squinted to focus, everything suddenly changed. I was somewhere else.

Now sitting inside of an enormous bathtub, I noticed how six or more people could fit inside. A tall white candle was placed in each corner and as the flames flickered about, each one cascaded little shadows upon the walls. The bathroom was beautifully covered in crème stoned tiles; everything was immaculate.

Sitting beside me was my baby boy. He was all of two years old, small, but was such a happy little guy. Jumping up and down, he was slapping the water with his tiny hands. His bursts of laughter were contagious and my heart melted while watching his perfect, little sweet face. I was surely one of the happiest and proudest moms alive.

When I looked across the tub, my oldest son was sitting there staring at me. He was around three and half years old and his eyes of brown were full of love. When his smile spread across his beautiful face, I sat in a state of awe. These two little guys were my pride and my joy.

But then, I noticed someone else in the tub, too. A woman. She was sitting next to my oldest and I didn't feel like I knew her very well. She had dark brown hair, almost black, and her brown eyes matched her long locks. Her face was gorgeous and flawless, and her eyes could see right through me.

Her name was Judy and she was there to help. Her job was to teach me how to rid the poison from my children. Ah yes, that's right, I remembered. She's here to help me bathe my kids.

My boys needed to be washed with a special soap mixture in order to remove the poisons they were covered in, and she was there to make sure I did just that.

I was young; in my early twenties. I had long brown, feathered hair, bright green eyes, and was tall and slim. Even though I felt educated, maybe in this area of expertise I wasn't, and that was the reason for Judy being there.

After reaching to the right and picking up the plastic bottle, I poured a large amount of the liquid substance onto the cloth. Setting the bottle on the side of the tub, I lathered the special potion into the washcloth, receiving Judy's approval.

Before I could place the bottle away, it slipped from my hand and dropped into the water. Instantly, I knew I had made a very big mistake. The potion was ruined. As quickly as I could, I grabbed it up, but the water had already mixed in. Pouring more of the substance onto my cloth, I tried to clear the water from the mixture.

Little Pauley, my youngest, was having a great time sitting beside me. He was splashing the water, making a lot of noise. He absolutely loved getting a bath and also loved to sink underneath the water, too. Every time he'd spring up, I'd act surprised and then watch the excitement light up his face. His giggles were to die for—he had the best laugh ever.

Pauley's little hand was tugging at my arm. He wanted to play and go under the water. I responded to his plea, "Only for a second, son, and come right back up, okay?"

Happily, he sunk below. As he did, I quickly turned and placed the bottle of potion high enough on the ledge so the kids couldn't reach it. When I turned back, my focus remained on rolling the washcloth and lathering it up the best I could.

In my peripheral vision, I saw Pauley still under the water. Fearing he'd been there too long, I instantly reached in and grabbed him by the arm, swiftly pulling him up.

My fear was correct, something was very wrong. For one, the color of his skin was horrifying and secondly, his entire body was stiff as a board. I couldn't fathom how this had happened.

What I knew for sure was I needed to get help, fast. Pauley wasn't breathing and he needed CPR immediately; I didn't know how to administer it. Deep within, I knew there was no help for him, but as his mom, I had to do something. And then it hit me.

"Judy can help us!" I screamed.

Instantly, I glanced across the tub and saw no one there. What I did see, however, was dark movement below.

"Oh my God! She's under the water, too!" I said franticly, never thinking once it could have been my oldest son.

Reaching over, I grabbed a handful of hair and pulled as hard and as fast as I could. Because of her weight, I knew it'd be more difficult to pull her up. But strangely enough, it wasn't as hard as I imagined.

When the small body of my first born leaped out of the water, I shrieked loudly because he too, was stiff as a board. I panicked.

"How did they get this way?" I screamed. "How long have they been under the water?"

The length of time for the boys to get this way, stiff, wasn't registering inside my head. Shaking with fear, I jumped up and tried gaining my balance. After placing Pauley's hard body under my left arm, I then grabbed my oldest son and placed him under my right arm. Screaming at the top of my lungs and as fast as I could, I raced through the bedroom to the outside world.

"Someone help me!" I pleaded. "Please! I need someone to help my kids. Please help us!"

My entire body jerked with fright. I was wide awake...

My heart was beating fast. The fear inside my chest was strong, close to exploding. Her voice was screaming inside my head, still.

"Help me! Someone please help me!"

Unexpectedly, a very strong presence in the room appeared. It wasn't bad enough being scared, now I was absolutely freaking out. Scooby and Angel started acting funny, barking at nothing. Deep, deep fear flew in and took over every thought I had. Someone was trying to get my attention.

Convincing myself it was just a dream, a bad nightmare, wasn't working. Recently, I started to physically feel things in my sleep and when I did, I acknowledged it as being ten times more real. When those babies fell into my arms—they were very stiff. And when I tucked them next to my skin, the lifelessness of their bodies was indescribable. This was much more than just a dream.

It was freaking real and extremely intense.

There was no chance for sleep after that, so I decided to get up. *I need coffee, really bad.* The kids were taken outside to potty, but all they did was bark at nothing. An hour later, even after a shower, their insistent behavior to shout was worrisome. They could see things I couldn't—I knew that—they had become my eyes to the unseen and I trusted them completely.

It was time to ask for safety, so I did. A few minutes later, the shield of protection could be felt and it was only then, that I knew everything was going to be okay. Calmness had taken over that creepy crawly fear, finally.

What I couldn't figure out was how that lady lost track of everything. The young woman had no clue, none whatsoever, of how much time she had lost. As far as she was concerned, she turned to place the soap bottle up on the shelf and the next thing she knew, she was lifting her babies up out of the water. And the Judy lady—where did she go? More importantly, who was she?

Using the internet as a tool, I searched for a timeline on *rigor mortis*. What I found was that it starts to set in at three hours after death, with full rigor at twelve hours. After the twelfth hour, it begins to cease and at around seventy-two hours, it disappears.

The two little boys... full rigor mortis. Twelve hours.

I kept them all a secret though, never sharing the dream with anyone or even looking for help in deciphering. Instead, I documented them. In short, I thought if anyone attempted to interpret, they'd remove the young woman's experience and claim it to be a symbol of a suppressed emotion. I didn't see it that way.

The woman was entirely too real to be a submerged feeling or emotion and to put it simply, I wasn't going to allow someone to take her, or her baby's lives, and turn them into something they weren't. I was an overprotective mama.

Six months later, I found myself conversing with a very good friend, Colleen. She, too, was a medium. Having met Colleen also on Facebook, it wasn't long before we became good friends and oftentimes spoke on the phone.

Before I knew it, I was on a mission and spilling details

about this particular dream-visit. Whenever I did something like that, share something I saw in a dream, I always took it as a *sign*—a sign that it was time for me to find *the* answer.

In this instance, Colleen was the chosen one. That in and of itself was interesting because in the past, I had never asked her for information nor received a medium reading from her; we were just friends.

Colleen asked, "When was this, the date of your dream?"

"I think it was in June," I replied.

"Would you say it was before or after the Gulf Spill?"

"It was right before it, I think," I told her. "I'd have to go and look up the date in my notes."

"Okay. I want to say—when you were talking about toxins, and being on the beach, and toxins were along the fence, in the house—what I kept getting was in regards to the Gulf Spill. That's what I'm getting. So you were having like a—even though you didn't understand it while being in the dream at the time—it was their way of presenting a forthcoming event. I'm being shown this was a precognitive experience. Even if the spill had already happened."

"Well, that makes sense," I said. "The whole dream was about chemically-based toxins, and it was very bad. The young woman was supposed to be cleaning it off herself and her children. But I don't know who the Judy lady was. It was like she just disappeared. I guess what I figured when I woke up, thinking back on it, I thought she had something to do with the death of the mother and the two children."

"Well, what I get is that she's your spirit guide," Colleen said. "She was just there to act out—did act out—in your dream. And I have to say her job was to get the message across, get her point across. As far as the two babies and the toxins—you use the word toxins many times—what I'm getting is that we need to be more careful even with the products we purchase and use on ourselves. In other words, watch what we're dumping down the drain or what's going down the drain."

She paused a moment before continuing. "In relation to the time-frame the lady was feeling—time isn't the same on the other side. What seems like hours to us, is only seconds for them. Your guide, removing herself and getting out of the loop—I want to say she was demonstrating their response time. She was demonstrating to you—the process of washing away the toxins—this is what's going on. People are *not* on top of things. People are not listening closely. Not looking at what they should be looking at."

"The message I'm getting from this dream is based on the toxins, the chemicals. I know how upsetting this visit was for you, but this woman was only spirit. She was playing a part in your dream. She was trying to make a point which wasn't so much about the kids, the point again is, we need to be more careful with what we're using and what we're doing."

Colleen's explanation was quite surprising. Obviously, I wanted it to symbolize something else. The physicalness of the dream felt important and a clue to pay attention. I could see it... Spirit used the physicality to keep me engaged.

Right after Colleen and I hung up, I remembered that odd essence in my home upon waking that morning. Maybe I brought someone back with me, from the dream world. That would certainly explain the dogs barking and once again, both worlds coming together, colliding. Judy was there, with us; I'm convinced of it.

Because I can't see them, spirit, I creep out easily. Sensing them is easy, but not knowing who they are, spooks me. Hollywood has done such a good job instilling fear of the paranormal, they've ruined it for true spirit communications. It was a *big* job retraining myself not to fear what I couldn't see, and an even bigger job trusting that my gatekeeper would allow *nothing* to harm me.

Judy was masterful; she made sure I got it. Colleen's message may not have been what I had expected, but it was still incredible insight. Years later after this conversation, while scanning my notes, I found an amazing surprise about Colleen.

During the same discussion, Chip's death was briefly discussed. At that time, the murderer was still free.

Here's what Colleen said:

"I'm being told you will hear something important about Chip in the next six to eight weeks."

I asked, "About his murder case?"

"Yes," she responded.

Honestly, her comment was pushed under the rug along with several others who had predicted an arrest. Two and a half years after Chip's murder, nothing had changed. Believing that justice would ever be served—that was fading, fast.

And then the murderer was arrested on September 23, 2010. Colleen was right on the money. Exactly six weeks and five days after our conversation about the woman and her children, the killer was finally behind bars.

Chapter Eighteen

The Missing Girl
Chip's Work

S ecretly, I wished for those same gifts my new friends had; to hear and see the other side as well as they did. Because of the vast amount of dream-visits, I began to believe I had something, albeit not the same as their gifts.

There was a point where I actually convinced myself that my connection with mediumship was through dreams.

That thought was promptly removed before it really had a chance to grow. I knew we had something special. It was easy to recognize this marvelous connection between me and Chip. Grateful, appreciative, and thankful, will never come close to what I carry in my heart for the Afterlife.

I was, and still am, addicted to their love.

It was earlier in the year when Megan shared something new about Chip. She told me that he was showing her *how* he was helping souls cross over, and then she described his job on the other side, too. She said the uniqueness of his work was in the *who* he was helping.

She said, "He works with the senseless deaths and the senseless murders. Young people not understanding the depths of their immaturity and recklessness while causing their own death through accidents. Children being murdered; souls who when they flipped out of their body might be freaking out saying *what the f****. These are the people, the souls, he connects with and helps to cross over."

It was perfect, and right up his alley. I knew Chip would be good at his work and it'd be something he'd love and be destined to do. What I didn't know back then however, was the possibility of being *shown* exactly how he worked.

It never dawned on me, not once, that Chip could bring someone to see me. Or that I might slip in somehow to see him while he was at work. I had no clue he could include me and show me how he helped souls cross over.

Because the visits were amazingly real, much more than the physical world, I held a secret compartment of *hope*. The kind that someday in my dream state, he'd give me information that would crack the case and find his murderer speedily arrested. I should have known better.

While my broken heart continued to heal from his physical disappearance, I failed to remember one important message— do **not** focus on the murder, rather, focus strictly on him.

But I so badly wanted to help find evidence and assist Chip to rest easier—or so I believed. In the end, I learned it was me I was trying to help, not Chip. What I wanted and what he wanted, were two entirely different paths.

Educating myself was a long and tedious process.

I don't always get what I want, but I do get what I need.

Over time, the dream-visits changed. They weren't filled with rich love as before and some of them had me scratching my head hard, taking longer to figure out. When their importance was recognized though, the magnitude of their design was completely understood and the appreciation for what they were, *divine*, it was powerfully inspiring.

Chip Oney had his own agenda. I simply played the role of a grieving widow communicating with her dead husband, who by the way, took her on the ride of her life. Through fascinating scenery, beautiful landscapes, tangible and physical acts, we wandered throughout the universe in a magical bliss.

The next chapters convey visits and descriptive messages and a few of them, depict Chip's assistance to the souls traveling back home. Around this time was when I learned the value of the gifts I had received—Chip's job in the Afterlife.

The Missing Girl
Chip's Work

It was a late morning on a dreary Saturday, when a nagging headache pounded relentlessly behind my right eye. It simply wouldn't go away, crippling me from everything and forcing me back into bed.

After napping, I slowly dragged myself up and headed to the kitchen for a drink. As I entered the hallway, a sudden rush of visions encapsulated my mind. As quickly as they appeared, so too did my voice as it slammed against the walls.

"Oh, my God! Chip has a missing girl with him!"

The intensity of that statement blared loudly, causing me to do an about-face and run straight to the computer room. Everything had to be documented and completed as fast as I could type it. It felt extremely important.

"I must remember every detail," I told myself.

So I began to type…

Standing in unfamiliar territory, I could hear my lingering thoughts as they tried catching up with my surroundings. As I sensed the proportion of the room, I also noticed a couch butted up against a large picture window. It was rectangular in shape, extra-long, and framed in a shiny dark cherry wood.

A glass-top coffee table was positioned at my feet, in front of the couch. I was standing still, frozen in place, in the middle of a very small living room.

"I don't know this place," I detected. "Nothing around me looks familiar. It's certainly nothing I own."

As I looked around trying to grip my reality, a loud sound suddenly grabbed my attention. It was my cell phone ringing from the right-side of the room. My purse was sitting on top of a counter ledge next to a microwave.

"I don't remember putting my purse there," I whispered. "Where the hell am I?"

After grabbing my phone, I held it out to read the caller id. It said, ___ Bread Shoppe. The number wasn't displayed but the city was; Laurel, MS. Normally, if I don't recognize the number, I won't pick up the call. But something inside was telling me to see who this was. Timidly, I answered.

It was my father's voice on the other end. Because we rarely talked, I was stunned it was him. The few times a year we did chat, I made sure to tune in and give him my undivided attention, just like now.

"Hey, baby," he said. "Listen, I don't have very long to talk. I need for you to check on something for me. It's really important. I need you to ask your ex a few questions about a missing girl he has hanging out with him."

I was shocked, but still responded, "Okay."

Confused, I questioned who he was talking about. I knew he had to be speaking about Chip, but Chip wasn't my ex.

"So who is he referring to?" I wondered.

"Are you still there?" Dad hollered.

"Of course I am," I answered, "You scared me a little, that's all." And then I lied, "I'm trying to find something to write with, so you can give me her name."

Scrambling quickly, I searched for paper and pen in my purse. But the desperation I heard next confused me even more.

"We don't have time for that," Dad shouted. "He's on his way to you. Right now!"

Click. My father hung up; he was gone.

Blankly, I stared at the phone. Standing more puzzled than when I had arrived, my dogs appeared out of nowhere and started play fighting. My Chihuahua, Charlie, was throwing food at my Chihuahua, Angel. I knew instantly that Charlie had passed away, but it didn't seem to faze my reaction.

"What? Dogs can't throw food," I sensed something very odd happening. With my hands on my waist, hip cocked to one side, I yelled, "What's going on here?"

At that exact second, a small light glimmered inside the window. Squinting my eyes now, I swore I could see Chip's truck. His big red Dually Dodge was traveling around a bend far off in the distance and then out of nowhere, sudden happiness draped itself over me like a big blanket of love.

"That's Chip," I mumbled.

The bend wrapped around a large mountain and in the darkness behind him, hills homing thousands of trees were dancing in the wind. As I watched the soft orange and pink clouds float across a dark blue sky, I could hear a silent voice. It was telling me that I was standing inside a living room of a small motel, located high up in a mountainous area.

At the same time, Chip crossed the road directly at a wide curve and was headed straight toward me. I watched as he pulled into the parking lot, then up to the window, and then came to a stop. The headlights of his truck were beaming so brightly, I had to look away.

The dogs were still playing, fighting with each other, and being very loud. Charlie had gotten the best of Angel and I feared him hurting her. Upon breaking them apart, I started to scold little Charlie.

"No. Bad boy," I pointed my finger. "You can't do that to Angel. She isn't trying to hurt you. You're being a bad boy..."

The door flew open in mid-sentence and I quickly lifted my head to see who was there. My scolding came to a rapid close as I whispered, "a bad Charlie."

Chip had unquestionably startled me when he speedily dashed through the door. Our eyes connected, but all I could do was vacantly stare. It had only been seconds since he pulled up to the window, and now, he was right in front of me.

"How'd he do that?"

As I stood, my shorts suddenly fell below my knees. Fumbling to retrieve them and pull them up, I noticed my attire. I was wearing a very long, white shirt; certainly not something I owned. I was grossly embarrassed.

After I grabbed the shorts and yanked them up—they were his red boxers—I noticed that Chip was talking; I saw his lips moving. In all of my awkwardness though, I hadn't heard anything he said.

My head turned quickly toward the big picture window when I had to do a double take. It was one of those moments when I knew I saw something, but I wasn't sure if I saw what I thought I saw. There was a young girl sitting behind the steering wheel of Chip's truck.

Instantly, I was thrown into utter shock. My stare must have been noticeable because out of the blue, I could hear Chip's voice clearly leap through my concern.

He said, "She's only here for a little while. She'll be going to her family shortly. I'm only looking out for her, helping her."

His tone was filled with admiration for the young girl.

As I turned back to look at Chip, I noticed now that he was standing next to the door. Trying extremely hard to absorb everything that was happening and just as Chip did, appear so quickly, the young girl did the same darn thing. In a flash, she bounced hurriedly through the door searching for Chip.

When she saw me though, she stopped dead in her tracks and stood motionless, staring into my eyes. I wasn't sure if she was as shocked to see me as I was to see her, or if she was shy and scared of what I might do.

Out of habit, I instantly began to assess her.

She had to be in her young teens because she didn't look a bit over the age of fourteen or fifteen. She was thin, about five-foot-six or seven, and had short brown hair. She was wearing an extremely soiled tee-shirt and a pair of very short shorts—the daisy duke kind. She was filthy dirty and desperately needed a good bath.

Before I could evaluate anything else about her, she darted out the door. Keeping her in my line of sight the best I could, I watched as she jumped back up into Chip's truck. Tightly, her fingers grabbed the steering wheel as she peered over it, staring directly at me. Sensing this girl's giddy and trusting behavior, I knew that all she wanted, was to drive the truck.

She bounced up and down in the seat, smiling ear to ear, jerking the steering wheel back and forth. Nothing else mattered, she was ready to go.

"But she can't be old enough to drive," I questioned.

Turning quickly to face Chip again and ready to ask him a

dozen questions about the girl, I was stunned to see him right in front of me. He pulled me into his arms and hugged me extra tight. Wrapping mine around his back, I peered over his shoulder looking for the girl. I couldn't stop thinking about her.

"Why is she driving your truck, Chip?" I asked.

He pulled back, wrapped his hands around my face, and then gently kissed me on the lips. As he let me go and stood tall, he slowly started to walk backwards. A large smile decorated his handsome face and now, I couldn't take my eyes off of him.

Each of his shoulders lifted toward his neck and then he dropped them, saying a silent, "I don't know." His left arm reached out and grabbed the doorknob. When I found his eyes one last time, he said, "Youth. Whatcha gonna do with 'em today?"

In an instant, everything went black and Chip was gone.

The next thing I knew, I was standing inside of a parts store. I was working there and either my father owned the place or he operated it. Two young black men walked in and asked for assistance. Their car wouldn't start and they needed a jump. My dad was very protective and also very insistent.

He told them, "You will need to call someone who can help you. We have no means to assist."

They didn't leave though. They knew we owned the car outside the shop and they wanted us to help them by jump starting theirs. My father once again apologized and told them we had some place to be and were already running late. They still didn't leave, so my dad then allowed them to use the Yellow Pages and the desk phone to seek help.

As my father headed to the back of the shop to lock up, he leaned down to whisper in my ear. "As soon as they're done, we have to leave to go to the post office. You make sure you lock up the front."

As the young men talked on the phone, I grabbed a keychain with a butterfly decal and walked to the far end of the store. Bringing the key up to lock the door, I noticed it was brand new and bright gold, too. "Is this supposed to have a meaning?" I whispered, wondering why it wasn't silver. "Will it lock the door?"

After inserting the key, it turned with great ease. I then headed back, right as the two young men had completed their phone calls. Very politely, I asked, "Can you please step out of the store so my father and I can leave now?"

Ryder had come to their rescue and it cost them eighteen dollars for the road call. I remember their car being a white four-door sedan and I recall vividly, the guys seeming to be nice on the outside, but very mischievous on the inside. They were teenagers, about eighteen or nineteen years old.

In the blink of an eye, I was suddenly standing at the front door of my home, trying desperately to lift up the glass portion of the screen door. My sister was with me, watching. The glass was getting stuck for no apparent reason and what was even crazier, was all the plastic wrapped around it.

Peeling away layer after layer at a time, I was trying to clean the glass so I could lift it up. As I removed it, I turned to look at my sister.

I told her, "I've had this one song stuck in my head all day and I can't get it to leave."

"What's the song?" she asked.

Turning to pull away more, I started to sing the lyrics.

"When the moon is in the seventh house, and Jupiter aligns with Mars. Then peace will guide the planets, and love will steer the stars. This is the dawning of the Age of

Aquarius."

Unexpectedly, her voice took over and I stopped singing. Taken aback, I couldn't help but stare at her, amazed that her voice sang so beautifully.

"Harmony and understanding, sympathy and trust abounding. No more falsehoods or derisions, golden living dreams of visions, mystical crystal revelation, and the mind's true liberation. Aquarius."

She knew the song and even more surprising, she sounded like an angel. Inclined to sing with her, I turned to finish the peeling project and once done, I lifted the glass door as it snapped loudly into place.

After locking it, I gazed and stared out at the driveway.

My body bounced and my eyes flew open.

It took only seconds to realize I was lying in bed and the headache from earlier was still pounding hard. I slowly dragged myself up and headed to the kitchen for a drink. As I entered the hallway, a sudden rush of visions encapsulated my mind. As soon as they appeared, so too did my words as they crashed against the walls.

"Wow, that was wild. Hey! I saw you, my darling, and I touched you. I *felt* your lips against mine."

A few more steps and I decided to announce my gratitude. With a sincere, raspy tone, I said, "Thank you for coming to see me, sweetie. Thank you, thank you, thank you." I looked up and then said, "I love you, my darlin'."

Once in the kitchen, I pulled down a glass from the cupboard and that's when it happened. That's when the light bulb moment hit me like a ton of bricks. Shouting loudly, even startling the kids, I was filled with surprise.

"Oh, my God! Chip has a missing girl with him!"

Jabbering like a little kid, I couldn't shut up.

"Oh no, Chip. You have this girl *with* you, don't you?"

I waited for an answer, but heard nothing in return. I knew the dreams were important and suddenly, I became filled with concern. So I asked another question.

"Okay, what do you want me to do with this? Is there anything I can do?" Again, there was nothing but silence.

I started to pace the floor.

"Damn it, Chip, you didn't give me her name. What am I supposed to do?"

Instead of waiting for another dose of silence, I turned and raced to the computer room. Everything had to be documented and completed as fast as I could type it. It felt extremely important.

"I *must* remember every detail," I told myself.

So I began to write...

All of those dreams, one right after the other, I truly thought Chip wanted something to be done with them. Once I broke them down, a great deal of information had been given about the death of the young girl.

Because she was covered in dirt, I knew upon waking she had been murdered. It seemed as though she had either been dragged through mud or quite possibly, buried in dirt somewhere. If she was buried, I had to believe she was partially wrapped in plastic, too.

I'll never know for sure, but I believed there was a connection with Laurel, Mississippi, and a Bread Shoppe, too. Because of the song my sister and I sang, I had wondered if the young girl was an Aquarius; born in late January or possibly early February.

According to the dream itself, it was highly suggested that the two young teenage boys kidnapped the young girl and murdered her. Whether she worked at the auto parts store with her father was unknown. The dream could also be interpreted as this father and daughter sharing an experience with these boys and in doing so, they could identify them.

I didn't necessarily believe the later interpretation simply because of the gold butterfly keychain. For me, butterflies symbolized transformation. Since the dream made a point in showing that, it made more sense to acknowledge that the girl transitioned into the Afterlife. She was a brand new butterfly... meaning, she had recently released her physical body and was now in spirit.

Months went by before I accepted I could do nothing. The only thing Chip wanted me to do with this information was to embrace the experience, as well as his work and his love, too.

Who knows, maybe someday someone will read this and connect the dots. Maybe they'll know exactly who she is and quite possibly, her family will find comfort in knowing their baby is okay. They'll be comforted knowing she was very well taken care of during her transition. They'll know she was allowed to do whatever she wanted when she passed because my sweetheart, Chip Oney, made sure of it.

He may have been keeping an eye on her but he also made her crossing as exciting as he could. Looking back on it now, it's easy to see how she had Chip wrapped around her little finger. She tugged at his heart and whatever she wanted, he gladly obliged.

What a blessing to be able to share his *work* through my writing. What an honor to be allowed to see how beautiful his heart is and bear witness to how openly he continued to share his love.

Sincerely, I was lost in *bliss*.

Chapter Nineteen

In Another Body

And God said, "Let there be light" ~ Genesis 1:3

"*M*y eyes were glaring at my feet. I was wearing camel-colored steel-toed boots and was walking through a lot of dust. Trying hard to focus, I looked up to see where I was going. The powder was flying everywhere and tons of drywall was lying about.*

Trotting through a busy construction site, I somehow knew exactly where to go. I was carrying files for new hires and my job was to interview the applicants, or at least I thought it was. Everything was still too dim and I wasn't sure yet about my role.

"I think I'm here to hire contractors to complete a job we've been assigned to," I said, under my breath. "We work together—wait a minute, where on earth did I get this 'we' from?" I questioned.

And then it hit me, Greg, my old boss. My eyes shifted to point him out and then I whispered, "Greg's my supervisor." I nodded and then affirmed, "Okay, that makes sense."

I walked into a small trailer that was being used as office space. As soon as I stepped inside, I knew instantly that I interviewed the contractors and then recommended them to Greg. If he approved, he'd put them to work. So far this morning, we had hired two.

At the moment, I was studying blueprints laid out across a long platform table. I heard the door open when a female entered the office. My head may have been lowered, but I sensed a very strong-willed woman walking toward me. Her presence was unmistakable.

She stood tall, confident of her abilities, of her skills as a carpenter. She had an attitude filled with desire and I sensed a drive for success that emanated from her Being. It didn't take long to look through her application, to briefly speak with her, before I knew how perfect she was for the job. I recommended her to Greg and he agreed, assigning her to a project at the other end of the building.

And then she turned sideways.

She was proudly walking past me, shoulders back, her head held high when I saw it. It was so vibrantly obvious, her baby bump. My heart dropped clear down into my stomach.

She was at least five or six months pregnant. The unfortunate part for her was that my boss saw it, too, and headed directly for me.

"She can't work here!" he demanded. "You have to let her go." As Greg walked past her, he shunned her and that really disturbed me. Before I knew it, a few more people had done the same thing and in only seconds of time, this poor woman had become a misfit with no one wanting anything to do with her. I couldn't figure it out. Was it because she was a woman performing a man's job? Or was it because she was pregnant and suddenly unwanted?

I was terribly sad. And I still had to break the news to her.

After I did, I turned and followed everyone else's lead and

walked away from her. Staring down at the floor, head held very low, filled with embarrassment and ashamed of myself, I watched my feet move forward.

A nagging thought raced inside my head. Sure, I felt a great deal of sympathy for the woman, but I also felt a very determined question mark, too.

> *"What if she's God made up into this woman? Do I dare leave her like all the others did, stranded without help? Is God watching me to see what I'll do? Is he testing me by being her and waiting to see if I keep walking?"*

I couldn't be sure. The one thing I did know—I never wanted to be the one who disappointed Him. Just by my questioning this, it was proof enough for me. I wouldn't turn my back on her. She needed my help and without delay, I walked back.

"Do you have any place to stay?" I asked her.

Her head dropped slowly as I watched her eyes dart across the floor. Very shyly, she shook her head back and forth, no. I reached out to grab her hand into mine and waited for her eyes to lift back up.

"Come with me," I told her. "We'll find a place for you to stay. And we'll get you something to eat, too."

We walked out together, but as we left, everything went dark.

My eyes were extremely fuzzy and with all my might, I couldn't focus. I knew for certain I was lying in my bed, but what I couldn't quite figure out, and what I couldn't see yet ... "who was that standing beside my bed?"

It took a few seconds before my vision returned. It was the same woman I helped earlier. She was there, standing beside my bed.

"Hey, baby doll," she whispered. "It's me, your Chip."

"What? Are you serious?" I couldn't believe my eyes. I was filled with disgust and extreme irritation, too.

"Are you trying to play with my emotions because I helped you?" I demanded an answer.

"No, no. It's really me, Chip," her voice ripped through my head. "I promise you, it's me. The owner has been very gracious and has allowed me some time to enter her body so we can talk. Just like you asked for, remember?"

But I couldn't believe any of it was real. She was lying to me and I didn't understand why she wanted to hurt me like that. I wanted her to leave. She was a very, very cruel woman.

"That's ridiculous," I called out. "You can't be in someone else's body, Chip. And this isn't funny. I need for you to leave. Right now!"

But she begged, "Ask me something, anything, so I can prove to you that it's me. Anything."

She sounded very sincere and gradually, I started to dance with the possibility. I realized if I was going to be an open-minded person, I should at least play along to learn if it was true or not.

So I decided to think of something recent and something I knew this woman could never know. Possibly something that happened yesterday and only Chip, no one else in the whole world, could know.

"Okay," I said sarcastically, "What did I ask you last night while I was outside taking pictures?"

She instantly replied, "You asked me what it was like to be next to the stars."

I rose up into a sitting position so fast, you would have thought a fire had been lit underneath me. I stared deeply into her eyes.

"Chip, it really is you, isn't it?" I posed.

She smiled and nodded her head, yes. An instant rush of exhilaration swallowed me. I wanted to ask Chip how it could be, how he could do this. I had a ton of important questions I needed to ask, but on the other hand, if it was him, I didn't want to waste our time squabbling over petty questions.

"How long can we talk?" I asked.

"We've got four hours and then I'll have to go."

"I can't believe this," I was so excited. "Well, I don't want to stay here in bed. I seriously need a cigarette right now. Let's go outside and sit."

The next thing I knew, we were sitting in the rockers on the back porch, rocking back and forth, with everything feeling peaceful and just as it should be. It was still dark out and the slight breeze was cool, not in the least bit chilly; it was perfect. There wasn't an ounce of eeriness to anything going on and all I felt was complete joy and total comfort. I couldn't believe it, but I was indeed sitting there, allowed to talk to Chip, in person.

"Why did you hide your smoking from me when I was here?" he asked, breaking up my thoughts.

"Because I didn't want you to gather a negative opinion of me for having such a bad habit," I told him. "I thought I could deal with it. And if you didn't see me smoke, you couldn't get upset with me."

"I could never gather a bad opinion about you, my darlin, ever," he said. "You were the one solid in my life and because of you, I was happy."

"You know I love you very much, right?" I never wanted him to question my love.

"Yes, I do," he confirmed. "And you know how much I

love you, right?"

"Yes. I do." I tilted my head back and steadily rocked, feeling a tremendous amount of peace. Chip was there! He was right there. Nothing felt different and nothing had changed between us. This was us and it was fantastically real.

"Good," he calmly said. "Very good."

A brief moment passed before he spoke again.

"We're okay, baby doll. We're okay. We've got much more work to do, but please don't feel like it has to be done all in one day. It will take time. And yes, to answer your question, we are working on everything. When it's the right moment, you will know."

All of a sudden, I felt something moving underneath me. The ground was shaking. I quickly placed both hands onto the arms of the rocker, and hung on for dear life.

In a flash, I was wide awake. My big ole Scooby had walked across the bed and caused the ground to shake. My immediate reaction was to get him to lie back down and be still. After he was settled, my reality finally caught up and that's when it smacked me.

"Is Chip still here?" I jumped out of bed, kids in tow, and ran to the back porch. Upon opening the door, I looked out at the rocking chairs and that's when I said, "No, he's not here."

It didn't take too long to start questioning the visit.

"Wow! Did that happen here? Or did that happen over there?" I couldn't be sure.

It was *that* real. I knew it happened, whether it was here or not, it most certainly happened. Both worlds colliding, again.

"That was insanely good," I smiled. "I think I need some coffee."

Chip had a big dream and one he insisted we'd fulfill some day. He shared it with me so many times, I began to love it as much as he did. I can still hear him tell it.

He said, "You wait and see, baby doll. We'll be in our seventies, old and gray, walking around with our damn canes and sitting on our front porch rocking in our rocking chairs. And when we get there, we'll rock and we'll talk about the good ole times we had together. I promise you, too," he'd tap my leg twice, "I'll share everything you've been curious about." (His Navy secrets.)

He'd then grab my hand from his lap and lift it to his lips, softly kissing my fingers. Curling our hands together, he'd press them both firmly against his chest and then ask, every single time, "Sound good?"

It sounded perfect to me. I wanted it to happen for us, too. And for tonight, it did.

Somehow, someway, he made it all ... *come alive.*

Chapter Twenty

At Work

with Katie Starnes

"Chip's work seems to be with people who pass suddenly and don't understand what's happened. It's the accidents, and the murders, and when they die they're dazed and confused saying, *what the f***.*"

"It feels like the young boy was drinking, there was alcohol involved, and maybe he borrowed his dad's truck. He lost control, and wrecked, and died. Chip is there, helping him cross."

Dazed, I couldn't believe what I was hearing. This wasn't a déjà vu, this was a grand validation. With almost identical words, I was told the same thing Megan had said months ago about Chip's work in the Afterlife.

The pattern was forming and I could see it now. These weren't *I love you* visits, these were, *Chip's at work* dreams.

Holding my cell phone, I watched my fingers dial *67 while calling Chip's home. It was obvious I was hiding my number hoping he'd answer my call. I wanted to surprise him.

The phone rang twice and then, unexpectedly, it stopped.

Nothing was said and there was no hello. A few seconds later, a surprised female voice said, "It's Lyn." And then shockingly, I heard Chip's mom's voice, too.

She said, "Don't answer it."

I gasped in shock as I removed the phone from my ear and stared at it in disbelief. "Did I just hear what I think I heard?" As I halfway listened to the conversation on the other end, my thoughts explored her rude comment. Thinking this woman loved me like a daughter, I was very confused and hurt.

But then I heard her give details about things I had done for Chip, things I was doing and even things I would do in the future, for him. I felt her love for him and her joy too, as she spoke about Chip and me. I beamed inside.

I heard a loud click and suddenly knew the call had ended.

Hastily, my fingers dialed another number, still trying to reach Chip. It was important I talked to him tonight. Instead of hearing the phone ring this time, I found myself at one of my old jobs, the one in fact, where Chip and I first met.

There wasn't any furniture to speak of in the office, but it didn't seem to matter. I was visiting old pals and was delighted to see everyone there. Chatting on the floor against the wall with a friend, I glanced up in front of me when I spotted a new window overlooking the front drive.

"That wasn't there before," I reflected.

The window was enormous with a small box-like frame, covering the entire wall from ceiling to floor. The glass was remarkable and the visibility was amazingly clear. I swore it looked like no barrier existed between inside and the outside.

Out of the blue, a red Dodge pickup turned into the entrance. "It's Chip!" I cried out. My full, undivided attention was instantly centered on that truck. Everything was moving in perfect slow motion, too. My zooming ability was like off the chart, I could see the entire passenger side up close and personal.

Unexpectedly, the color changed and the truck went from red to blue... just like that. I jumped in my seat and questioned silently how that could happen, but there was no time to think about it. There was more to observe in front of me.

The truck was a deep, dark, blue color and it had been damaged to holy heck and back. The entire rear-side panel of the bed was mangled. It was in horrible shape and shouldn't have been allowed on the road.

"Why is Chip driving a wrecked up, should be totaled, hunk of junk," I wondered, out loud.

The wheel well was completely smashed and now I could see that the entire side of the truck looked like it was beaten with a sledge hammer. It surely had to have taken a tumble or two to be so badly battered.

"It's (the truck) not as big as Chip's dually," I whispered.

As it drove to the oversized window, I gazed up into the windshield. There he was, his handsome-self sitting behind the steering wheel. Instant jubilation rushed through me at once. I was so happy to see Chip and I couldn't wait to hug and kiss him all over. I had missed him madly, I felt that inside.

Glancing toward the passenger side and back, I noticed a young man sitting directly next to Chip.

"Well, that's odd," I said. "He's practically sitting in Chip's lap." The young man wasn't on the passenger side of the truck, not even close.

Our eyes met and I smiled at him, but he didn't smile back. Hell, he didn't even blink. He was frozen in time, staring blankly, making it almost impossible to feel anything from him. Yet he didn't seem, or feel, scary to me.

"Maybe he's scared," I said. "Who is he to Chip? Do I

know him? Is that my brother, Billy? No, it can't be. He bears no resemblance."

My head rocked with questions.

"Who is this guy? Why is he sitting right on top of Chip? Why isn't he sitting closer to the door? Why is Chip feeling mad? Wow, Chip is really pissed off, I can feel his anger. Is he mad because I'm here?"

*"Hey, how did I get here?" I asked, looking around now. "And **why** am I here?"*

Jerking back to look out the window again, I located the young man once more.

I yelled, "And who is this kid?"

Cocking my head to the side and thinking, I tried to estimate his age. He appeared to be between fifteen and seventeen years old. I broke our stare for a second to take a peek over at the passenger seat in search of more answers. There was no one else sitting in the truck.

Unexpectedly, Chip budged. His body shifted and I moved my eyes over to watch him. He opened the door, stepped out, and then walked fast, very fast, to the office entrance. When he entered, his anger engulfed me. It was so thick, it galloped through me. I couldn't help but be startled. I hadn't ever felt him like that before.

"I know I haven't done anything to upset him, but dang, he feels really mad about something." I refused to move. "What in the world did I do to make him so angry?

The manager's office was closest to the foyer and Chip opened the door and moved in. When he closed it behind him, I suddenly knew he was there to pick up his check. Exactly how I knew that, I wasn't sure. A few seconds later he marched back into the office area and then directly, didn't miss a beat, he proceeded straight out that front door.

Chip ignored me, completely. He never engaged in any kind of conversation and never acknowledged me. Oh yeah, he was mad, big time.

I watched him stomp his way back to the truck, open the door, and then slide inside. His hands grabbed the top of the steering wheel and his knuckles wrapped tightly around it.

When I beheld his eyes, he was already staring at me, peering over the wheel.

My body jumped and my eyes popped open; I was awake.

My heart was pounding fast in my chest, but I didn't waste a second of thought. I sprung right back to the young man.

"Why wasn't he sitting in the passenger seat?" I asked, out loud. "Is this supposed to be a clue?" I waited a few minutes for a voice with words, but I didn't hear anything back. Yet, his position in the truck felt like a big clue.

"Okay, so is this someone who is close to you in your family?" I was fishing. "Or possibly someone in mine?"

I closed my eyes nice and tight and waited for an answer.

Nothing. Zilch.

The only thing roaming around were my thoughts. It didn't surprise me really. My head was too busy; I was in overdrive.

"I know there's a reason this guy was sitting so close to you, Chip," I said, staring at the ceiling. "I can't figure it out right now, but I know there's a reason for it. That young boy is very important to you. I just know he is."

Asking for help at this point in time wasn't something I did much of. For one, it wasn't right to bombard my friends with my many dream-visits and two, I needed to learn to interpret the visitation dreams myself. Besides, I was supposed to be growing in my journey and part of that growth should include my own interpretation to what I saw while sleeping.

I swiftly documented the details and thought about the

young boy constantly. Non-stop, he wandered inside my head with no luck in figuring out who he was. Not until a couple of days later, that is.

I was very surprised when I was asked to be interviewed to discuss my first book, *Wake Me Up: Love and The Afterlife*. Graciously, I accepted; I was very excited. Kate Starnes, the radio host, and I spoke on the phone before the interview.

Kate is a medium and the moderator of her own show, *Intuitive Skies*. Our chat was to be quick and discuss briefly the questions she'd ask so I could better prepare. However, our conversation took a rather big detour.

The topic turned toward lost loved ones and soon, she told me she had lost her brother and shared that he was around her always. When she mentioned him, all the bells and whistles went off in my head. *"Could it be? Could the young man in my dream-visit be her brother?"* The timing was too perfect and I felt the need to ask.

I told her about the young man who, only two days earlier, was sitting in front of me with Chip. With no warning, Kate delivered information I'd never forget. The young man in my dream-visit was not her brother, no, but the news she was about to share… was mesmerizing.

"Chip wasn't mad at you," Kate said. "He was mad at the boy."

My focus had become submerged into her voice.

"It's like he says to the boy, *I didn't have a choice. My life was taken from me. Now look at what I'm missing out on. You had a choice, but you f***ed up and blew it.*"

I was stunned! Literally and physically, dazed. My mouth dropped to the floor, wide open. It was clear as day; I could see it. Even if Kate didn't know what was transpiring, I *knew* exactly what was happening. This lady didn't talk this way.

This wasn't her style of vocabulary and didn't fit her personality whatsoever.

Who she did sound like though—was Chip. It was so him. I do apologize for his sailor mouth, but I swear he left nothing to the imagination. You never had to wonder where he came from because he laid everything out on the table.

If it was at all possible, Kate was channeling Chip. Because of this, I was flabbergasted and couldn't help but be captured. Every word she spoke, I burned like a CD.

"It feels like the young boy was drinking," she told me. "There was alcohol involved, and maybe he borrowed his dad's truck. He lost control and wrecked, and died. Chip is there, helping him cross."

Kate took a deep breath.

"His work seems to be with people who pass suddenly and don't understand what's happened. It's the accidents, and the murders, and when they die they're dazed and confused saying, *what the f***.*"

"This is when Chip steps in and guides them home."

There it was. Identical words I'd heard months earlier from Megan. This was further validating Chip's activity now. I sat quietly, but oh, so excitedly. My heart was beating crazy-wild, anticipating more.

"Wow, this is really strange," Kate said. "Usually when spirit comes to me, I get information to validate them. But Chip, he's just here, like I already know him. I get the feeling you went to him, you went to see him this time. He didn't come to see you."

"No, you definitely went looking for him," she paused. "Yeah, this is his work and he shows you sometimes, who he helps go home. Your love for each other is beautiful."

"And no, he wasn't mad at you," she reminded me again. "He was upset with the young boy. You felt his irritation with the boy."

Everything Kate said made perfect sense. It explained the shock the boy must have felt—his blank stare. It explained the irritation that Chip was feeling, too.

Something she said—it didn't dawn on me until after we hung up. At the beginning of the dream-visit I called Chip. Twice I dialed his number, trying to find him. I *never* shared that information with Kate. So yes, she was right, I did go to him. That was interesting for me because I never knew I could do that, not until now, that is.

The most surprising aspect of the visit was Chip's personality. It hadn't changed one bit. I guess I imagined when he crossed he became this ultimate loving Being. At least that's what I read one time and thought it was true.

The author painted a perfect picture of souls entering the Afterlife. They said we no longer live with irritation, or hatred, or frustration, or anger. They said we become *love*.

But I didn't get that here.

Instead, I felt every bit of Chip's aggravation with the young boy. He was upset because the guy mistakenly took his own life. I can see that now, but surely I didn't expect that.

Poor guy, he looked so scared and Chip, bless his heart, he didn't let the young man off so easily. At least not before realizing what he had done. I hope after I left, Chip took the young man fishing and made him feel more at peace. I'm sure he did.

The validation of Chip's occupation on the other side was wonderful, fantastic, phenomenal... there are no ideal words. The message Kate gave was better than magnificent. She gave me more confirmation in defining who, the specific groups of souls, Chip works with.

It was truly exciting to learn all of this, but at the same time, it was so sad understanding what his job was all about. It meant, of course, that he was working with those who died.

The mere fact in knowing these souls leave families behind; mothers, fathers, husbands, wives, brothers, sisters, children, friends, nieces, nephews... my heart felt very heavy for all of them. I understood some of the pain they'd suffer, and I knew how hard it would be.

Death, it's such a real life experience. And an altering one at that.

Chapter Twenty-One

Michael Jackson

"Hello, detective. I know this is going to sound a little odd, but please bear with me. Last night, I saw a man I think is connected with Chip's murder. He was in a dream, but he was more than just a man inside of a dream."

"I can describe him to you. I can tell you exactly how he looks. I was extremely close to his face and I saw what he was wearing. I think he's involved with Chip's murder. If nothing else, he at least warrants an investigation."

My speech was prepared. Determined, my plans were to call the detective in charge of Chip's murder case later in the morning. Having never experienced a dream like this one before, I knew upon waking I had to be ready.

Even if the detective didn't believe me, or even if he thought I was crazy, I didn't care. It was my turn to help, my turn to do something for Chip. If he put all of that time and effort into making me see what I did, then the least I could do was be willing to put myself out there.

Sitting in front of me was a small alien-like face. It was definitely a beautiful face, but it wasn't an ordinary one. Not like yours or mine. It was more childlike and even brighter than the brilliance of sparkling snow, it was covered in a glowing, vibrant white shade.

It appeared youthful and flawless but had no physical characteristics whatsoever. There were no age lines or wrinkles, just smoothness all over. I could see no definition of a nose or even a mouth for that matter. Yet it was certainly a beautiful creature I was straddling ...

"What? I'm sitting on top of it?" I couldn't believe it.

As I gazed down, I could see that I was indeed on top of this beautiful Being. As I rejected the thought to move, I realized I knew who it was. Leaning in closer, I placed my face directly in front of theirs and stared, hard, refusing to blink. All of my attention was placed where this gorgeous and captivating Being's eyes, should be.

Suddenly, one eye opened and I jerked, slightly. The corner of its mouth broke into a half smile as I cocked my head. I knew exactly who it was.

"Chip, I know it's you!" I said with amazing confidence.

Instantaneously, the transformation happened right before me. He turned into the Chip I knew and recognized. Lying underneath me with a huge smile, he certainly thought he had outwitted me.

"Why do you continue to disguise yourself like that?" I asked. "You know I'm going to figure you out."

He broke into a loud laugh. So boisterous I almost had to cover my ears, yet at the same time, it sounded divine.

"Because it's fun," he roared. "I like trying to fake you out."

Like a tidal wave, it hit me. "Chip's here!"

The exhilarating rush physically sailed through me.

"It's really him. He's here, he's really here."

It felt like ages since I'd seen him and my enthusiasm took control. Lunging forward with all my might and wrapping my arms around his neck, I held onto him as tightly as I could, while I made an odd humming sound.

Next, I pulled myself back and grabbed each side of his face and held him firmly. I then started plunging my lips all over and smacked him with each smooch. I kissed his head, his cheeks, his nose, his eyes, his mouth, and then I did it all over again. With each kiss I placed upon him, I emulated the sound, "muah."

*"Muah, muah, muah," I uttered, kiss after kiss. I couldn't stop myself, I was so happy to see him and too, he felt **so** good.*

A few minutes later, I leaned down and started kissing his neck, still muahing him, while I listened to his laughter. I didn't care if he thought I was being silly. My focus was to caress him with my lips. He had been terribly missed.

Moments later, I rested my head on top of his shoulder and gently, kissed his neck. I was in heaven and felt so much love. No matter what, I knew I didn't want Chip to ever leave me again.

"Okay darlin'," his voice startled me.

His tone was loud and jumped right into my wandering and happy thoughts. He had quickly garnered my attention.

"I need you to stop for just a minute," he said. "I have to check out what this is, on top of my head."

"On top of his head?" I questioned. "He's not going to find a bandage there. He's been healed for a very long time."

Obliging his request though, I lifted myself from his neck as he grabbed my shoulder and gently leaned me back. While he guided me past his head, his left arm raised high into the air, patting the top of his crown. But when I looked, there was nothing there.

After squatting in front of him, I noticed he was sitting on top of an old brick wall. Bright green grass was everywhere and large beautiful trees swayed behind him.

And then something completely out of the blue came into view. It was horrible and I swore my eyes were deceiving me, they had to be. There was no other explanation for it. Because what I saw in front of me... was unbelievable.

Chip's hand was covering the tip of a gun.

I froze in place and declined every thought to move. I seriously couldn't accept what I was seeing.

I asked myself, "What the hell is happening now?"

Appalled at this entire situation, I knew I had to watch every move Chip made. Suddenly, everything became like a wide-screen movie on TV. Once the complete image positioned itself in front of me, I noticed another man had entered the picture and was standing beside Chip.

Chip's hand was wrapped around the barrel of the gun while this man held it. The gun was pointed at Chip's head. But after blinking, I saw the nose of the gun on Chip's head.

I became filled with caustic fear. Somewhere inside, I knew I was going to lose him another time. I could feel it. This stranger was going to murder my sweetheart, and Chip was once again, going to disappear.

With a fierce amount of focus, I watched the man with intensity. His every move and every action was being recorded through my eyes.

And then his head slowly turned.

The stranger was looking at me, smiling.

"What the hell? He has the audacity to smile?" I told myself. I was beyond disgusted and deeply sickened. I did not smile back. Absolutely refused to.

In the last few minutes, I made a snap-judgment that this

man was connected to Chip's murder. He was the other person involved in Chip's death and now, I was being shown this new information so I could help. My inner self was finally helping me to solve the grandest of grand puzzles because gun, always equals clue.

Fixated on the stranger, I no longer focused on Chip. Everything was about the other man now. Chip was showing me something important and no matter what happened here, I was going to pay attention. At last, it was my turn to help.

The stranger took a seat beside Chip as I watched them talk back and forth. They carried on like they'd known each other for long time, and this suddenly threw me into a confused loop of turmoil.

"Why are they talking like they're best buddies?" I asked myself. My head was racing crazy fast and I couldn't hear a word they were saying because my mind wouldn't shut up.

"I don't get it."

A couple of minutes later and after watching them act like nothing was wrong, I questioned their sitting together.

"Crap, what if they're friends? What if in some other lifetime, Chip was friends with this dude?"

I brought myself back quickly though, "I don't care!"

"If this man had anything to do with Chip's death, I'm not at all happy about it. If Chip forgives him, that's all well and good for him, but I'm still here and I'm not happy about any of this shit."

Chip leaned over to the stranger and bit a chunk of flesh from the side of his face. Somehow, that didn't gross me out. At the same time, like magic, my eyes had an amazing ability to zoom in. The stranger's face was sitting perfectly in front of me as I studied him, hard, taking lots of mental notes.

"There's no chunk of skin missing. Huh, that's weird. He's

not white, but his skin color isn't black either. Is he Indian? Okay, note to self: his skin color is different, odd, I can't put my finger on it."

"Look at his hair," I said.

"His hair is long, chest length, black hair. It's not smooth or even shiny. No, it's long and stringy—dark, dark black hair."

"This is good," I affirmed. "I need to call the detective when I wake up. He needs a complete description of this man so a search for him can begin. This is him, I just know it is. Chip wants me to find this man."

"Okay, Lyn," I said out loud. "You need to make a mental note on every detail about him. Look to see what else you can get that you know you'll remember."

I dug in by studying his facial features further. I started by looking at his forehead and then followed a path past his pointy nose and made a special note about his full, pinkish lips. When I reached his chin area, he startled me by standing up.

"His jacket is incredibly loud," I observed.

Still talking with Chip, the stranger stood tall as I took a camera shot of his coat. It was the deepest, darkest, purple I had ever seen. It was a leather zipper jacket and was fastened closed, up to his neck. Directly next to the middle zipper were two more, one on each side.

Unlike regular zippers, these were especially wide and nothing like I'd seen before. Their color was the brightest of gold that sparkled like glitter. They were all very loud, almost to the point of being obnoxious.

The brown color at the waist of the jacket confused me. It wasn't made like the rest of the coat and it wasn't leather either. It looked more like yarned-up suede. The wrist area and the neckline, too, all had a brown suede material, yet it was barely noticeable against the deep purple. It was actually quite attractive.

"Why am I completely engulfed in identifying this darn jacket?" I asked myself. "Stop it, right now!"

Abruptly, the stranger turned to face someone's arrival. In that moment, I sensed a lot of people around; there was a party going on. The man started to mingle with the new crowd while I stayed focused on his stupid jacket.

There was a zipper on the back, as well, trailing from the very top of the neckline down to the waistline, centered. On each side of the centered zipper were two more, intricately stitched diagonally. All of the them were fastened closed and all of them were the brightest of gold.

"I know purple symbolizes royalty, but I wonder what gold means?" I asked myself.

The stranger suddenly turned and was facing me when I noticed how tall he was. "He's got to be all of six feet if not taller, and he's skinnier than a bean pole. Seriously, he needs to gain a few pounds. I almost feel sorry for him, he's so thin."

As he walked toward me, I found myself staring at the pants he wore; old, black jeans.

"Man, this guy is all legs," I said.

Much to my surprise, there was no sudden jerk in my body. Instead, I was wide awake. I didn't want to be here on this side, because I needed to complete my investigation. I needed to gather as many details as I could about that stranger.

But that wasn't going to happen. I remained still, eyes closed, and remembered every feature I could. It felt really important to do so. I also devised a plan.

Later in the morning, I intended to call the detective of Chip's case and inform him about this strange new man. I would share with him what he was wearing, what he looked like, and hopefully sit with a sketch artist, too.

Since I couldn't go back to sleep, I got up and followed my morning routine; taking care of the kids, talking to sister, and drinking my first cup of coffee. When I got into the shower, my quiet space to think, I had it all figured out. Knowing exactly what I wanted to say to the detective, I rehearsed my speech out loud.

"Hello, detective. I know this is going to sound a little odd, but please bear with me. Last night I saw a man I think is connected with Chip's murder. He was in a dream, but he was more than just a man inside of a dream ... *it's the man in the mirror, oh yeah, make a, change* ... I can describe him to you. I can tell you exactly how he looks. Wait, what?"

"Were those lyrics smashing in with my thoughts?" I questioned loudly. I waited to hear something back, but nothing was said.

Dropping my arms and letting the warm water run over my back, I started to travel in another direction. Those few words had startled me and now I wondered if I should change my course.

"Why that song?" I asked. "It belongs to Michael Jackson, right?" And then I answered, "Yes, yes it does."

"Is it possible?" I looked up. "Can it be? Was that man I saw with Chip, Michael damn Jackson?"

"No!" I shouted. "It can't be true."

That stranger was not Michael Jackson, I was certain of it. Chip didn't know him and surely, he wouldn't bring MJ for a visit. It just didn't make sense and so it was settled; not MJ.

Needing it to be perfect, I returned to my prepared speech. There wasn't a doubt the detective was going to think I was crazy, I accepted that, but I still needed to use words to make me look sane.

"I was extremely close to his face and I saw what he was wearing. I think he's involved ... *it's Michael Jackson, silly* ... with Chip's murder. If nothing else, he at least warrants an investigation."

"What? It's Michael Jackson?" I hollered.

"Did I hear that right?"

It was official. I felt crazy!

I quickly wondered if I made this up and inserted words that didn't belong to me, and mixed them in with my own thoughts. I truly believed that stranger was not Michael Jackson; no way, no how. Instead, he was the man who helped murder my Chip. Period! End of discussion.

"Chip! Stop messin' with my damn head!" I yelled out.

A few minutes later I couldn't help but question if I should've been open to the possibility. After getting out of the shower, I voiced my concerns to Chip.

"Okay, let's assume it's possible," I said. "For the sake of this argument, let's say he was MJ. If he is, as you say, that would mean you planned the entire dream, right?"

I was on a mission and heading somewhere for sure.

"So, if you orchestrated this dream from start to finish, then you planned to scare the hell out of me. What's more, somewhere along the line, you would have acquired a really sick sense of humor, too. I'm not so sure I want to believe, sweetie pie, that you had a hand in all of this."

Because I didn't want to believe he choreographed the visit and intended to scare me by having a gun pointed at his head, I chose to believe he showed me the second party involved, in killing him.

And so it was. For a while at least...

As soon as I arrived to work, I hit the internet highway.

Googling every conceivable *Michael Jackson purple zippered jacket* way, nothing came back as a match to the one I saw hours earlier. After searching for more than an hour, I found a jacket that looked somewhat similar that had been worn by Andrea Kremer in 2009, but it wasn't identical. At the time, Andrea was a sideline reporter for Sunday night football.

Not even the authentic *Thriller Jacket* matched the one this man wore last night. But they were moderately related. It didn't really matter though, because nothing had changed. My determination to contact the detective was still moving forward. However, before I dialed the number, I decided to go over my prepared speech one more time.

As I spoke the words out loud, the light bulb moment struck me and the whole idea was heard clearly; it sounded insane. Picking up the phone wasn't going to happen anymore than sharing this dream with the detective, *ever*.

That morning, I learned something about myself … I had a one track mind when it came to Chip. If I saw a gun, I thought *clue*. When I saw someone murdered, I thought *clue*. When I saw horror and felt frightened, I thought *clue*. It didn't matter what he showed me in my sleep, I always thought *clue*.

Clearly, he had a sick sense of humor now. But if he knew I'd only pay attention to what I thought was the *clue*, then what better way to take me there, that way. Chip knew if I saw a gun pointed to his head, it was going to scare me into remembering. And he was right.

Later that evening, I called Megan. If anyone could make sense of this experience, it would certainly be her.

"Remember how intent I was on remembering Billy's chocolate brown pants?" I asked her. "That's how this one felt too, except this time it was the purple jacket. Can Chip really be hanging out with the one and only Michael Jackson?"

"Gotta love that," she said. "When I was doing readings for assistants to celebrities, I met a lot of famous people over there. I don't remember who they were, guess I should, but it was something like, *gosh he reminds me of Liberace*, and the person would say, *no, that's probably him*. I'd be like, *holy shit, I'm talking to Liberace!*"

Yes, indeed. I could relate.

Holy shit, I met Michael damn Jackson! Sweet!

Chapter Twenty-Two

Evidence Of Bliss

A fter the second Christmas without Chip, it had finally sunk in. He really was gone. The sadness was still kicking me at times, but what amazed me more was the contact we still had with each other.

I didn't have him here to wrap my arms around, or to even carry on with a meaningful conversation, but what I did have, was his love and his constant companionship from that other side.

The greatest gift Chip gave me was *sight*. Not the kind seen with physical eyes, but the type of revelation where one knows and understands, with no reservations whatsoever, that being alone was never again a possibility.

He gave me the *miracle of life*.

After Chip's death clicked and his new life covered every avenue and pathway I walked, dying no longer scared me. And life, the beauty of life being the gift that it is, engulfed me. When I understood that I had chosen this amazing life, my views and opinions, my goals and wants, all started to change. The *knowing* that I had set myself up for success long before I ever set foot onto this gigantic planet, took my breath away.

We have this one life, this one big and beautiful life, and each day we awake, the miracle of our existence is *the* gift. We can experience it however we wish. Whether it be through the sounds of nature, or the sounds of spirit, or even the sounds of drama, the blessing lies within the experience of *living*.

I'm so glad I chose to live when I wanted to die.

It is beyond words the experience offered to us to continue our relationships with the people we love in the Afterlife. Chip shared many different types of signs and messages, but his favorite was to communicate through dreams. A few of the visits hijacked my heart and long before I thought about writing a second book, I knew what its last chapter would entail. Because it was also a birthday present, it made it that more special. I called it, *Evidence of Bliss*.

EVIDENCE OF BLISS

While sitting on the passenger side of an unknown vehicle, a rush of sudden thoughts entered my mind—we're on a very dark, secluded, and lonely country road. Looking out through the windshield ahead, I barely saw anything in front of me.

"We? Why did I say we? Who am I with?"

I glanced over at the driver and saw my sister holding the steering wheel. "Okay, change of thoughts—Sister and I are driving down a dark, empty road."

"Oh that's right," I whispered. "We're on a trip. But where are we going?"

I had no idea and couldn't remember a thing that happened prior to now. However, I did sense a huge inner knowing that I had recently eaten an egg sandwich. Yum.

"Ha! My fave, now that's funny," I said to myself. "What more could I have to worry about?"

Smiling at my silly inner-self, I now remembered that we had packed our lunches for the trip and knew our aim was to eat what we brought. Yet, a few minutes later, a small diner/store came up on the left side of the road when Sister stopped at the red light, turned, and looked directly into my eyes.

"Should we?" she asked.

Looking over toward the diner, I shook my head excitedly and said, "Sure, I can handle another egg sandwich."

We both laughed as she parked the car. After exiting, I added, "And some chips would be nice, too."

*As we entered the store, food disappeared from the agenda and instead, the need to shop materialized. For some odd reason, I needed to locate a new blanket showcasing Christmas decorations and it **had** to be hand-made.*

After walking into a very small room covered in hanging garments, I pulled a towel down and spread it out on top of a table. It was smothered in Halloween décor and even though it was beautiful, it wasn't what I was searching for. Truthfully, there was nothing catching my eye, so I exited the room.

There were dozens of people situated about when I sensed I was standing in Mary's shop. Mary was a mentor at my old spiritual church in Jacksonville. Instead of focusing on the people though, I anxiously sifted through another isle of materials sitting in front of me. I was still on a mission.

From out of nowhere, Mary appeared. I hadn't seen her yet, but I knew she was somewhere behind me. My intuition was validated when her voice skipped across my shoulder.

"So, Lyn, do you get any feelings about the twenty-fourth?" she asked.

It confused me a bit why she would ask about a certain date, but as I sorted through the garments and felt her presence walk around me, the words fell through my lips.

"Yes, the twenty-fourth," I said very confidently. "And the twenty-second, too."

As soon as I answered her question, I felt someone else standing behind me. This person began to massage the back of my neck and it felt really, really good.

"Chip's the only one who does this," I whispered. "But he isn't here in the physical world anymore."

It took a few seconds more before it hit me.

"Oh! He's here in spirit," I almost jumped out of my shoes. I knew it could be no one else. "How exciting is this?"

Having experienced his magical spirit massage several times in the past, I understood I'd be leaving on a trip, a fun-filled journey, very soon. This thing Chip did on my head—it was his sign to let me know he was taking me away.

Allowing myself to relax into his touch, I started to let go. As I tilted my head further back, Mary had finally come into view as I watched her walk in front of me. She must have seen something in my eyes, or something going on around me, that worried her.

"Oh my, Lyn," she shouted. "Oh my!"

All I could do was listen. There was no power within to fight what was happening, nor did I want to. I was paralyzed and feeling incredibly content, while Mary stood only feet away, watching. But the need to calm her fears affected me.

"I'm okay. This is an awesome feeling," I cried out. "It feels really, really, good. It's not bad. I promise, Mary."

Electrical sensations and subtle vibrations started traveling throughout my body. Over time, I had become quite addicted to this pulsating charge and somehow, if it made sense, I felt plugged in as it energized my essence. This was euphoria. Every inch of me was skipping with electrical magic and it felt miraculous.

My feet were unhurriedly lifting from the floor and slowly, my body started to spin in a circle. Thousands of colorful lights began to embrace me, rotating around me.

"Lyn, oh my," Mary shouted. "Oh no!"

But no amount of concern was going to stop me now. This was going to happen. On the third spin, I was gone, no longer inside the small diner.

My eyes were bound, but my feet were moving. I couldn't see anything around me, but I knew I was walking. Fast. Step after step and at a very fast clip. I felt a little uneasy and a little dizzy, too, and as hard as I tried to gather all of my senses, nothing was coming together as quickly as I wanted.

My left arm was held tightly while I was guided to move. Suddenly, a small voice spoke inside of my head when it said, "You're walking arm-in-arm with Mary."

With Mary? What the...

Like magic, the ground below clearly appeared. We weren't in Jacksonville anymore, that was obvious. I had no idea where we were but what I did know, this place was very different.

Suddenly, my fingers came alive and I felt them clasping the sides of a hood on top of my head. I could tell I was clearly trying to keep my face hidden. Instantaneously, a strong knowing came over me, "Do not look at your surroundings!" But nosy me peeked anyway and when I did, I saw only the grounds. Nothing was recognized.

There was a strong desire and need to hurry. We weren't supposed to be there-- at all. It seemed forbidden. We could get into a lot of trouble if we were caught.

"Where exactly are we?" I pondered.

The grass was bright green under my feet and off in the

distance, white buildings were lined up one after the other. None of them had windows. A basketball court sat in a corner, detached, and empty of anyone playing.

Only one man was seen walking around outside. He reminded me of a guard or someone who was protecting the terrain. Yet, as soon as I saw him, Mary reprimanded me. She told me to put my head back down and keep moving.

The land seemed far, far away. So far away, no one even knew it existed. It felt so different there and unlike anything I'd ever seen before. And silence... it was extremely quiet.

Steadily moving forward, side-by-side, we continued to hold our heads down. Several minutes into our march, I felt lost and became very concerned for our well-being.

I whispered, "How do you know where we're going?"

"We keep going this way," Mary whispered back. "If we begin to go the wrong way, someone will step in and guide us into the right direction."

A sudden breeze caused my hood to whip the side of my face and for a split second, I caught a glimpse of our attire. We were wearing cotton-like, crème-colored cloaks, with extra-large hoods. I swore they reminded me of a monk's robe.

Grabbing the side of the hood and lowering my head again, I proceeded as told. We had gone so far and for so long, I started to question what it was we were doing and where we were headed. So I decided to take another quick look around.

Just as I popped my head up, we had arrived at our destination. A very large steel door was in front of me when Mary told me to pull it open. We entered together.

We walked into a waiting room that seemed quite similar to a doctor's office, but there was no sign of a physician anywhere. Searching for magazines, papers, anything really, I saw nothing but a round table. It was located about twenty feet *away near a door that seemed to lead out into an enormous hallway.*

A woman stood with her back to us, speaking to someone at the opened door. As I stared at her, wondering who she was, Mary suddenly gripped my arm and guided me deeper into the room.

She leaned close to my ear and whispered. "Okay," she said. "You now have to ask her where you need to go, to sign in."

Happily, I rallied forward and approached the woman, but when I asked her where to go, she just looked at me and said nothing. A few seconds later, she changed direction, walked around the table, and then took a seat.

I sat across from her while Mary grabbed a chair behind me. The woman then looked up, and finally, acknowledged me.

"We've been waiting for you," she said.

Excitement dashed through me; I could feel the rush running through my veins. I never questioned why they had been expecting me. Instead, I kept my eyes focused on the lady, watching her every move.

When she lowered her head, I followed as she picked up a pen and flipped through a few pages of a very large book that was spread out on the shiny table. As she started to write inside of it, she articulated her penmanship at the same time.

"Lyn. And one guest," she said.

"Hey, I never told her my name, how does she know that?" I questioned silently.

Preparing to ask Mary about the oddity of this woman's statement, I turned to face her, but was startled by her sudden age; she had grown very old. Mary's arms were high above her head, swaying, and her mouth was wide open, laughing. She was as surprised about the woman's comment as was I.

"They know everything that we do," I whispered to Mary, and then I turned back around. The woman at the table—was very straightforward.

"I had a difficult time with this decision," she announced. *"When Chip asked me this past Friday to allow you to visit, I wasn't sure. But now I am."* She continued to write. *"He thinks you're really cute,"* she stated.

"Cute?" Shockingly, I responded. *"Huh."*

A little stunned by her cute comment, two thoughts were racing through my mind. One, a tremendous surge of irritation had grown for Chip. I couldn't believe he told this lady I was *"cute."* A hundred times, if not more, I had told him, *"If you don't think I'm pretty, don't tell me I'm cute. Cute is for a little girl."* Yet, he still insisted on using that word.

And two, I knew he wasn't going to think I was all that cute with the recent weight I had gained.

Out of nowhere, a man rushed through the doorway when all of my thoughts went missing. He was dressed in a short red and brown printed kilt. A very tight shirt wrapped around his broad chest, exposing his muscles. His arms were nicely defined, much more so than Chip's. All of five foot eleven, maybe a little taller, he was actually built quite nicely.

He reached out, grabbed my hand, and pulled me from my seat. With evident balding and much older than my sweetheart, he introduced himself as Chip's uncle. He had a beautiful Scottish accent that hypnotized me; he could do no wrong.

He had me as soon as he mentioned Chip.

It was unmistakable how much he liked to dance and when he suggested we do so, I was surprised I joined him. Doing a Scottish jig, skipping along a very long corridor, I was having a grand time. Several minutes had gone by when he decided to teach me a proper Scottish turn, too.

After practicing it more times than I could count, I performed it effortlessly. Even though I was extremely proud of myself, I never released the fact that I was dancing with a complete stranger. However, at the same time, I felt as though I had known this man forever.

I was having the time of my life.

I had no clue where I was and, quite honestly, I didn't care. There was something about being here that felt like home. There was one thing that caught my eye earlier in the reflection of a floor mirror though—I saw my feet.

For some reason, I was wearing the shoes I wore the weekend before Chip was murdered. We had taken his father out for dinner at our favorite seafood spot in Mayport—I hadn't worn those shoes since.

As much fun as I was having—laughing, twirling, tapping my feet and dancing in tune—it disappeared in a solitary flash. Everything... simply vanished.

Out of the blue, I was in a room with two twin beds staring at they're distinctive bedding of maroon. As I turned to look behind me, I noticed I was actually sitting on one of them; the one closest to the wall. I remembered specifically choosing this bed because it seemed safer; no one could come up from behind and scare me.

A young boy was lying in the bed in front of me. As I stared at him, I questioned whether or not he was there a second ago. He was awfully pale and didn't look very well.

Covered up in a pretty sky-blue blanket wrapped tightly around him, his face was the only part of him I could see. The blue blanket was pulled up to his neck and his head rested on his white pillow.

The hardwood floor was pretty and light blond in color. It was nice, bright, and very shiny, but there were a few dust balls under the window sill. The floor needed a good sweeping, but other than that, it wasn't too bad.

The walls were white and extremely clean. There were no markings, no hand prints, nothing really. Attractive blue curtains hung around the windows. Crystal clear, the windows sparkled as the sun shined in.

"Where the heck am I?" I questioned.

Out of nowhere, it hit me and I hollered it out loud.

"Oh no, I left Mary all alone! I just left her there all alone. I need to get out of here. I've got to get back to Mary."

The little boy suddenly moved in his bed and his leg lifted from under the blanket. As I turned to look at him, he sat straight up and stared directly into my eyes.

"She's okay," he said, in a very delicate and innocent voice. "She's been taken to her lighted loved one for a visit."

Instantly, I felt comforted and relieved. Because he made me feel safe, I never questioned how he knew Mary was all right. It was just understood. As I stared at him, I could see that his lips were moving, but I couldn't hear a thing he was saying. I tried desperately to listen, but nothing was computing inside my head. And then, out of nowhere, something moved out of the corner of my eye.

A woman was coming toward me.

She was slim with black hair. Beside her was a young teenager who I presumed to be her son. She entered the bedroom, walked around the little boy's bed, and then sat on the edge, placing herself directly across from me. Her son, the young teenager, took a seat beside her.

He reminded me of someone who had a rough life. His eyes were dull, very sad, and somewhat creepy-looking, too. He gave me the heebie-jeebies; so much so, I had to convince myself I had nothing to fear from him and I was safe.

His face was pale white against his jet-black hair and if I didn't know any better, I'd swear he was a real-life vampire. He was handsome, no doubt about that, but the paleness of his skin next to his dark clothing didn't help his complexion whatsoever. Decked out in black, he represented gothic wear superbly.

Once he was seated and I was convinced nothing would happen, I turned to his mother.

"How did you get over here?" I asked her.

Instead of telling me, she projected it and somehow, I saw remnants of information and events in her life that all led her to this mysterious place. Her son was murdered. He was a coin collector and the man who killed him was someone he trusted completely. The murderer wanted his coins.

Unwittingly, her son left a clue before he died. When everything settled down and she realized the police weren't going to help her solve the crime, she came across the clue. It led her to her son's killer and in trying to take matters into her own hands, she indirectly was harmed and ended up here, in this mysterious other world.

"I love my son more than life itself," she told me. "I would have done anything for him."

She turned to look at her son, raised her hand up to his head, and then gently brushed the hair from his dark eyes. Gazing at him like only a mother could, she said, "Including, killing his attacker."

"But knowing what I know now," she turned back, "I wish I would have done things differently. I realize I didn't help matters, I only hindered them."

Flash!

In the blink of an eye, I was somewhere else, yet still in this other-worldly place. The woman and her son had disappeared.

Standing in front of dozens of people, my eyes were searching for Chip's face in the crowd. Amidst my exploration, two distinct voices spoke out; I didn't recognize either of them.

The first one shouted, "Can you find him here in the crowd? Have you been able to locate Chip yet?"

Covered in goose bumps, the thought of seeing him sent jolts of electricity shooting through me. Chip was all I thought about, day and night. I missed him terribly and wanted desperately to see my sweetie pie. He was there, and those people knew he was there. I had to find him.

"Focus on the light of him, Lyn," the second voice said.

Rapidly, I searched for the face of that second voice, but he was hidden. He was talking, I could hear him clearly, yet I couldn't see him.

"We, all of us here, can see the light inside of you," the voice said. "We know you fear losing your light for Chip, and with this amount of time that has passed, some of it has dimmed, but not all. We know you fear forgetting what he looks like or even forgetting him all together, but don't worry, your light is still lit for him, and his for you. Focus on the light... you shall then find him."

I understood what he said—focus on Chip's light—I really did. As easy as it sounded, I had no idea how to do that. To comprehend that someone could focus on the light of a spiritual Being and then miraculously have them appear—how do you do that?

Going back to the only thing I knew, desire, I focused there. My want was to find Chip and now, I was getting a little worried that that wasn't going to happen. I had already looked at every face in the crowd and Chip wasn't there.

"I can't leave," I told myself. "I have to stay right here

and wait. Chip will find me as long as I stay right here."

Starting a second search through the many faces in the crowd, I suddenly noticed the silence. No one had said a word in several minutes, but there had been plenty of moving about. Maybe they did that so I could see past the next person and so on, I wasn't sure, but there hadn't been a single peep out of anyone for quite some time.

A few seconds later however, someone hollered.

"Let's go smoke!"

Instantly, I turned to face the man of the first voice.

"Smoke what, dope?" I asked him.

"Absolutely!" he replied. "We love to relax, too."

Curiosity took me by the hand and I walked with the crowd. I knew I didn't want to leave that spot for fear of missing Chip, but I had agreed to join them. And too, there was an odd knowing I felt within. Everything was fine and I was exactly where I was meant to be, with them.

The entire group turned in unison and headed up an incline toward a beautiful hilltop. Sweet, delicious, and magnificently bright greens entertained my eyes. Christmas trees were slowly swaying back and forth in the slight breeze, white and yellow flowers peeked throughout the hilltop, and sparkling tips of glistening snow sat quietly on top of the tallest of trees far, far away. It was simply... quite beautiful there.

Over to my left was rushing water flowing down into a gorgeous stream. It sounded like a gigantic waterfall yet at the same time, it was extremely calming. The graceful water sparkled like reflections of ice tips on shattered glass under a moonlit night.

Badly, I wanted to sit and wallow in the beauty but instead, I stood quietly, watching the dazzling water spank the boulder rocks in the middle of the stream. The only thing missing was a big wild bear attempting to catch its feast.

Suddenly, reality hit as I listened to my thoughts rushing in. "I really don't want to smoke with these people," I whispered. "I just want to go and find Chip."

In an instant, I felt everyone's movements behind me change. As I turned to look, a man appeared over the hill and was screaming something. On a very skinny road, he took extra-large steps while his arms swung wide.

He hollered, "Not here! Not today."

Everyone stopped what they were doing. In unison, once again, the entire crowd simply turned the other way and commenced to head back to where we had just came.

I cracked up laughing. I couldn't help myself.

This whole scene was hilarious.

It was so funny the way everyone turned around, at the same time no less, and traipsed away from the hilltop. I couldn't help but wonder why they hid the smoking.

"So you guys will get in trouble for smoking dope here on this side?" I whispered, to the man of the first voice. A few steps in, I felt the weight of someone else lean up against me.

"Yeah, but it's not the same kind of trouble as you know," the man near my shoulder said. "It's only frowned upon and that's about it. We like to keep the counselors on their toes, so we hide it. It makes it a bit more enjoyable here."

Everyone started to laugh... loudly.

Flash!

Again, like magic, everything vanished.

This time I was inside a bedroom sitting on the edge of a bed, waiting. Only seconds went by when I felt it again, the knowing. I was still there, in this mysterious other world, waiting for Chip to find me.

Very tired now, and ready for sleep, my eyes were feeling

quite heavy, so I decided to lie down. The man who I had been hanging with for the past few hours was resting too. From the corner of my eye, I saw his girlfriend lying over beside him.

I closed my eyes and tried to relax. Feeling much more comfortable in my new surroundings and with my back against this man, I let my thoughts direct my actions.

"A couple of minutes of shut eye won't hurt a thing while I wait for Chip."

Slowly, I started to doze away.

"Oh no!" I screamed, as I shot out of bed. "I can't go to sleep! If I drift off, I'll wake up. And God knows I don't want to be back there in that physical world. I must stay here and wait for Chip to find me."

Looking at my new friend and his girlfriend lying comfortably in the bed, I started to wonder, "Are they really sleeping?"

Getting up on my hands and knees, I slowly crawled toward them. And then over the top of them. Stealthily and like an especially good private-eye, I inched nearer while I examined them closely, checking out their eyes.

Searching for bouncing eye movements, R.E.M. sleep patterns, I sprung from one and then moved to check out the other. And then back again.

"Darn, they're sleeping."

Desperately, I wanted them awake.

"Hey," I whispered. "Are you guys asleep?"

Of course I knew they were, but I needed them to wake up. A second later, my man friend opened his eyes and turned his head to connect with me.

"Yeeeeessssssss," he comically drug out. He then closed his eyes and turned his head back. He was so funny, and a faker, too.

"Okay," I dispiritedly responded. I was still crouched across them when out of nowhere, a question popped into my thoughts. The need to know consumed me.

"So, do we require sleep over here?" I asked, believing this guy was still awake. Oh boy. They were both awake now.

They were lying together, still spooning, when the man lifted his head to look into my eyes. But he seemed a tad irritated with my question.

"Of course we do," he assertively replied. "We need rest just as much as you do. We're no different than you." He paused for a second before he added, "Not really."

A ton of questions rapidly surfaced. An explosion of fireworks burst in my head and the nosy me was front and center. There was no stopping me.

In preparation for more to come, I scooted to the end of the bed and was ready for anything, for everything. Crossing my legs Indian style, I propped my elbows on my knees and stuck my chin in the palm of my hand. Staring directly at them, I was now prepared to hear it all. I wasn't budging until I did.

They were taking so long to get up and I was becoming so impatient at the same time. Unable to wait another second, I just had to say something else.

"So where exactly are we at?" I asked them.

The woman unhurriedly rose from the bed, dragged herself away from her man, and slowly scooted toward me. My eyes were glued to her every move. The anticipation was killing me as I waited to hear her say something, to say anything.

She slowly positioned herself in front of me and then very calmly, her voice took flight.

"We are in Bliss," she softly spoke.

The sound of her voice was shocking. It was so soft and reassuring, it felt like music to my ears. If I didn't know any better, I'd swear she was an Angel.

As I sat with her statement, I started to get confused. My eyes darted off to the edge of the bed and then quickly back. I needed to confirm what she said.

"Bliss?" I asked.

"Yes, Bliss," she repeated. Again, I tried to rummage rapidly through my thoughts, eager to understand.

"Is this the place everyone calls Heaven?" asked I.

I really wanted to know this answer and knew I couldn't allow myself to get lost in some other thought. It was imperative I remained focused.

*"Yes, it is," she said. "But we call it **Bliss** on this side."*

She then lifted one leg up and allowed it to fall into place as she adjusted herself to get more comfortable. I was getting all bubbly inside, I could feel it, but I remained as quiet as a mouse hoping she'd tell me much, much more.

"Everything is the same, Lyn. We are the same," she said. Her soft voice floated in the air while her eyes lifted and moved back into mine.

"We feel the same things," she said. "We live the same way as you do."

"As you can see," her arm rose up and out into a beautiful but very slow, swan-like motion as she highlighted the setting around us, "it's all the same, Lyn."

"Nothing really changes."

Flash!

1-23-12

S tate of Florida vs. Colavito (Vito) Bell.
The trial began.
Guilty…

Ironically, the trial began four years to the very date that
Chip was murdered; January 23, 2012. It was a long and
grueling five days, but the end result was gratifying. The killer
was found Guilty of First Degree Murder.

That following April, he was sentenced to *life without
parole,* meaning the remainder of his physical life will be spent
in prison. That brought a great deal of peace knowing he can
never put another family through such horrendous devastation.

I've learned a lifetime of lessons since that dark and
dreadful, Wednesday morning. I often wondered if I would
have known then what I know now, would I have made it as
horrible for myself as I did?

Would I have made it as terrible for Chip as I did?

In my lack of knowledge and education about what
happens when a loved one dies, I failed to realize one

important component about life — death.

Whether my parents failed to educate me, or the schooling system failed to teach me, or even failing as an adult to discuss it, my obsolete views about death were most certainly a learned behavior.

I have to believe my reaction to Chip's rapid disappearance might have been different if I had been cultured about death in a spiritual sense. If somewhere in my life this was said, *death is a celebration for the one releasing the human body,* I would have had the *choice* to grieve another way.

If someone would have told me, *communicating with the Afterlife is a natural process and just because we die a physical death, that doesn't mean our soul dies, too...* I believe my grief would have been more about celebrating Chip's new life on the other side. Instead, the lack of education on my part only pressurized me into deep, unyielding sorrow, leaving me to beg daily, to die.

No one knows how they'll handle a tragedy until they're either in it or have already experienced it. Death, all deaths, including illnesses, senseless murders, freakish accidents, all of them, truly impacts the lives of those left behind. We are forever changed, forever altered.

Each of us has a path to travel when such tragedy strikes. Dependent upon the road chosen, miraculous adventures are sometimes experienced. At exactly 4:45 a.m. on January, 23, 2008, my awakening began, my new life about to start.

It is my unbreakable belief that when in tragedy, no matter the kind, if we can become aware, if we can re-train ourselves to feel, to see, and to listen to the divine messages being delivered, miracles *can* and *will* happen.

If we take it one step further and try to follow our loved

one's divine signs, follow our divine dreams, the possibility of physical creations manifesting, is much greater.

Dreams do come true…

"Dreams can come true…if we have the courage to pursue them." ~Walt Disney

"The future belongs to those who believe in the beauty of their dreams." ~Eleanor Roosevelt

"Dreams are more real than the perception of being human." ~ Lyn Ragan

The Afterlife has an amazing ability to communicate with our side. If I, the biggest skeptic of all, can do this, you can, too. When we listen, when we start searching for answers, and when we become one with our loved ones in the Afterlife, the existence we once knew… is no more.

Look for your *signs*. Search for your messages. They are there, right in front of you. Our loved ones leave signs as validation that they are always with us.

Love Lives Forever…

Chip Oney & Lyn Ragan

Acknowledgments

Without a doubt, I have been blessed to meet many beautiful souls the past few years. I treasure our friendship and thank you all for being in my life.

An enormous thank you goes out to all of the beautiful and gifted ladies who guided me into seeing the amazing proof of Chip's continued survival. You are all an inspiration, not only to me, but to everyone you touch. Megan, Leslie, Katie, Colleen, and Joanne — my deepest and sincerest gratitude. You are, for certain, Earth Angels.

A big thank you to my edit and review goddesses:

Author and Freelance Editor, Marley Gibson (Burns), *Author and Paranormal Researcher,* Dorothy Pigue; *Author and Producer,* Michelle Griffin; *Reiki Massage Therapist,* Pam Seavey; *Psychic and Medium,* Leslie Dutton; *Out of Body Expert,* Karen Doll; *Personal Assistant to Psychic Medium Chip Coffey,* Greta Refert; Julie Meers, *Ph.D., CHC;* my gifted mother, Mae; my second mom, Char; and my beautiful sister, Deb. Thank you, thank you, thank you!

To all of my family here in the physical world, and to all of my family and dear friends on the other side, thank you for loving me. To all of my Angels and Guides, I am eternally *addicted* to your Love.

And to the man I'll love forever, Christopher "Chip" Oney. My gratitude for your remarkable guidance and unconditional Love is greater than human words. Only you can hear the beating of my heart... *muah, muah, muah...*

Contact Information

To get in touch with any of the Intuitive Mediums listed in this book, use the contact information below.

1) Megan M. Riley – *www.MeganMRiley.com*
    Facebook: Megan.M.Riley0
    Email: mail@meganmriley.com

2) Joanne Gerber – *www.JoanneGerber.com*
    Facebook: psychicmediumjoannegerber
    Email: joanne@joannegerber.com

3) Leslie Dutton – *www.MagickBridges.com*
    Facebook: Leslie-Dutton-Medium
    Email: leslie.dutton@me.com

4) Kate Starnes – *www.IntuitiveSkies.com*
    Facebook: Intuitive.Skies
    Email: katie@intuitiveskies.com

5) Colleen West – *www.ColleenWest.net*
    Facebook: PsychicMediumColleenWest
    Email: c10@msn.com

To Reach the Author

Lyn Ragan — *www.LynRagan.com*
Facebook: WeNeedToTalkBook
Facebook: WakeMeUpBook
Facebook: BercsInnerVoice
Facebook: SignsFromTheAfterlife
Email: Lyn@lynragan.com

About The Author

Lyn Ragan knew at the age of fourteen she would write a book one day. She subscribed to *True Crime* and *True Detective*, reading each edition faithfully while plotting her fiction novel she never wrote. Twenty-five years later, she met the love of her life never thinking she'd be involved in a real-life crime. After her fiancé's murder, she followed his guidance by way of ADC's, (After Death Communications). From the other side, Chip insisted she write their story. Despite her struggles with grief and added defiance, she reluctantly gave in. Following Chip's communications, she penned their first book, *Wake Me Up! Love and The Afterlife*. Years later, Lyn was moved to write again. Encouraged to share their deepest connections, she intuitively used his words as inspiration and titled their second book, *We Need To Talk: Living With The Afterlife*. While writing her novels, Lyn was introduced to the spiritual arts of energy work. She pursued meditation intently and went on to study Reiki Healing, Auric Energies, and Chakra Balancing. She later used her studies to become a professional Aura Photographer, a publisher, an Ordained Minister, and a children's book author. Lyn enjoys sharing her afterlife experiences with Chip and hopes their story will help shed new light on continuing relationships with loved ones passed. She lives in Atlanta with her fur-kids, Scooby, Chipper, and Scooter. Lyn can be found online at *www.LynRagan.com*, and on Facebook at *WeNeedToTalkBook*.

CPSIA information can be obtained at www.ICGtesting.com
Printed in the USA
LVOW07s2345170315

430916LV00027B/1435/P